P9-CQM-248

The Student Leadership Training Manual for Youth Workers

*Everything you need
to disciple your kids
in leadership skills*

Dennis "Tiger" McLuen
& Chuck Wysong

Youth Specialties

ZondervanPublishingHouse
Grand Rapids, Michigan

A Division of HarperCollinsPublishers

The Student Leadership Training Manual: Everything you need to disciple your kids in leadership skills

Copyright © 2000 by Youth Specialties

Youth Specialties Books, 300 S. Pierce St., El Cajon, CA 92020, are published by Zondervan Publishing House, 5300 Patterson Ave. S.E., Grand Rapids, MI 49530.

Library of Congress Cataloging-in-Publication Data

McLuen, Dennis, 1953-
   The student leadership training manual : everything you need to disciple your kids in leadership skills /
Dennis "Tiger" McLuen & Chuck Wysong.
      p. cm.
   ISBN 0-310-22797-6 (pbk. : alk. paper)
   1. Church work with youth. 2. Youth—Religious life. 3. Christian leadership. I.
Wysong, Chuck, 1958- II. Title.

BV4447 .M374 2000
259'.23—dc21   99-053469

Unless otherwise indicated, all Scripture quotations are taken from the *Holy Bible: New International Version* (North America Edition). Copyright © 1973, 1978, 1984 by International Bible Society. Used by permission of Zondervan Publishing House.

Seven Styles of Evangelism is adapted from *Becoming a Contagious Christian* by Bill Hybels and Mark Mittelberg. Copyright © 1994 by Bill Hybels and Mark Mittelberg. Used by permission of Zondervan Publishing House.

Edited by Laura Gross, Lisa Baba Lauffer, and Sheri Stanley
Cover and interior design by Paz Design Group

Printed in the United States of America

00 01 02 03 04 05 06 / CH / 10 9 8 7 6 5 4 3 2 1

To my incredible kids—Sharri, Ryan, Mandy, and Bree, who all demonstrate their faith in their own ways and have shown me student leadership in action. I love being you dad, and I'm proud of each of you.

And to my wife Sue. Thank you for your partnership with me through these years of ministry.

—T.M.

To my mom, Rosemary Wysong, who was the greatest example of a leader I have ever known.

To my wife, Gale, the nicest person I have ever known.

To my childern—Stephen, Tyler, Benjamin, and Grace, my greatest inspiration. I love you.

Finally, to my prayer partners—Jon Ireland, Matt Mills, Walt Hansen, Greg and Linda Caruso, Russ Michealsen, Casey Cobeli, Renee Curtis, and Janel Getskow.

—C.W.

The Student Leadership Training Manual

Contents

Contents
(continued)

Acknowledgments

Special thanks to—

Glen Avon Presbyterian and Lakeside Baptist Church for giving me room to grow in youth ministry.

The staff, students, and alumni of Youth Leadership. Each has contributed to this ministry, encouraged me, and forced me to wrestle with important leadership issues. I am honored to know them.

—T.M.

Peninsula Covenant Church, Deer Grove Covenant Church, and Ocean Hills Covenant Church—three churches that caught the vision for equipping students and investing in student leadership.

Ray Johnston, who modeled, inspired, and taught me the value of developing student leaders.

—C.W

Contributors to this project: Dave Ambrose, Mick Baker, Travis Blomquist, Wendy Carpenter, Les Christie, Melissa D'Alexander, Gary Gadinni, Heather Hultgren, Dan Jessup, Terry Linhart, Greg McKinnon, Joel Newton, Dave Rahn, Katie Rowan, Mark Schoolmeesters, Mike Steiner, Kim Stumne, Marg Tilleskjor, Kent Yost, and Heidi Zellweger.

Welcome to the Student Leadership Training Manual for Youth Workers

YOUTH Talk

" Three pieces of advice for youth workers. Youth workers who develop student leaders have quite a responsibility to carry out. Three crucial things you need to do—

Lead by example. Youth workers need to develop their student leaders not by what they say, but by what they do. By being a consistent example of a shepherd to your students (because, in essence, you are shepherding the students in leadership), they will have a better understanding of—and the potential to become—that type of leader. Whatever leadership role a student is stepping into, it would be good for that student to have a positive, adult example who will train not only with words, but also through actions.

Find mentors. Student leaders need solid, mature mentors. Regularly meeting with someone who is more spiritually mature accelerates spiritual growth. The value of this practice increases as the mentor holds the student accountable and encourages her in every area of life. The mentor needs to be someone the student respects. While every person could benefit from a mentor, for student leaders it's critical.

Teach the power of prayer. Lastly, students must be taught and encouraged regarding the importance of prayer. Students who have no prayer life are weak leaders. Prayer is one of the most important disciplines, and without it we have little communication with God. Instill the principles of prayer in students and be an example to them.

These three principles were crucial to me as a student leader. Develop these and develop strong leaders. **"**

—*Melissa Bree D'Alexander, college sophomore, Waco, Texas*

Our early years in youth ministry were filled with adult leaders doing things for the teenagers. Adults did everything for every event, activity, or teaching session. We both experienced changes in our thinking about this approach as we struggled to impact young people. As we began to work with college students in leadership, we noticed how much they were changed by the experience of significant leadership. It got us thinking about this area of potential.

We each began to experiment by involving high school students in some of the leadership roles for our activities. We learned to listen to their ideas and solicit feedback from them about what we were doing. Since nothing was written on the subject, we found ourselves creating things as we went. In our own ways, we each developed a deep commitment to student leadership. We learned to grow in ministry with student leaders. They got us started on the subject of this book by challenging us, disagreeing with us, encouraging us, and serving Christ alongside us.

What's behind this book?

St. Paul reminds us in Ephesians 4:12 that part of our job as leaders is "to prepare God's people for works of service, so that the body of Christ may be built up." And "God's people" includes teenagers.

The Student Leadership Training Manual for Youth Workers is designed to complement any adult leadership-training program you currently use. Every youth leader we know struggles with building a quality leadership team. We believe effective, long-term youth ministry requires the ability to develop adults and teenagers as ministry partners who are contributing members of your leadership team. Student leadership is a way that long-term impact can be made in the lives of teenagers. And that should be our goal.

Effective youth ministry is more than attendance statistics. "The bottom line in youth work is not how many kids are coming to your youth group," writes Jim Burns, veteran youth worker and author, in *The Youth Builder* (Harvest House, 1988). "The bottom line is where your kids will be in five to 10 years. Is your church preparing them to be Christian leaders?"

Student leadership training touches the lives of young people in ways that impact their futures.

Of course you know your situation and your students best. It should go without saying, but we'll say it anyway: adapt these sessions all you want. Skip a topic if you've spent a month studying it in detail with your students already. Spend extra time on an issue they find intriguing. If your team already is a small group, stay together for a discussion. The *Student Leadership Training Manual for Youth Workers* is a valuable tool. Make it work for you.

How to use *The Student Leadership Training Manual for Youth Workers*

This book is a comprehensive resource for developing student leaders. Part one is an essential component that will help you address the foundational issues involved in effectively developing student leaders. You can use this section alone or with your adult leadership team.

Part two provides training sessions you can use with your students. The first group of sessions (one through 14) covers general leadership issues that can be used with all student leaders. The next five sets of sessions correlate to five areas of student leadership: Peer Ministry, Peer Evangelism, Ministry Teams, Servant Teams, and Program Planning Leadership Teams (all are described, beginning on page 14). Use whichever sessions are appropriate to the type of ministry you're developing.

The appendix section includes additional resources that may be helpful, such as samples and articles to get you thinking.

The sessions are designed to take 40 to 60 minutes. The recommended format of these sessions includes the following elements: Team Building, Team Huddle, Team Study, Team Planning, and Team Prayer. In addition to the material in these sessions, you will want to include time to plan and tend to any specific housekeeping details.

Principles for developing student leaders

[rationale and methodology]

What Is Student Leadership?

Chapter

1

- Tashi's youth group has an extensive youth worship component. Over 20 young people volunteer to play and sing for Wednesday youth group events. They're now preparing for a summer ministry tour.

- Sarah has eight teenagers trained to be peer helpers. They have been through many hours of training and are now listed in the church bulletin as peer ministers.

- Kwan has young people helping all over the church. They run the sound system for every youth event, work on the newsletter, set up the youth room every week, take pictures, and do a PowerPoint presentation after every big event.

- Across town, Casey has a passion for peer evangelism. He has set up a ministry that is calling young people to share Christ with their friends and on their school campuses. He provides peer evangelism training and has equipped a core group within his youth ministry. These students pray for their friends regularly, discuss evangelism strategies, and are held accountable for sharing their faith. Their Wednesday night program has changed to become more evangelistic and the energy around this issue is contagious.

- Meanwhile Jamalia has developed a group of seven teenagers who meet with her and two adult leaders monthly to help evaluate and plan the youth ministry program. They're held accountable to be at events and assist in the implementation of many of the ideas that were discussed at the youth board meetings. Students have applied for the one-year positions, attended a training retreat, and signed a leadership covenant. They're making a significant difference in the youth program because of their dedication and extra involvement.

Definitions of Student Leadership

A student leader is any student who has a desire to walk with God and influence other people.
—*Barry St. Clair*

These students exhibit leadership and integrity to others and are respected on their campuses for their faith.
—*Bo Boshers and Kim Anderson*
Student Ministry for the 21st Century

Teens at the develop [student leader] level are students willing to take the initiative, not only for their own spiritual growth, but for the spiritual growth of others as well.
—*Duffy Robbins*
Youth Ministry That Works

Student leaders take both the responsibility and initiative to reach their friends for Christ and help them grow in Christ.
—*Dave Rahn*

Student leaders are committed young people who are intentionally following Christ, and in doing so are leading their friends.
—*Tiger McLuen*

Tashi, Sarah, Kwan, Casey, and Jamalia are all excited about their student leadership programs. They all have student leaders, but their programs look totally different. It's important to be aware that there are many different ways to get students involved in leadership and service so you can be intentional in applying the student leadership models that best fit your ministry. Your church context, personal gifts, interests, current adult leadership, and youth ministry needs will influence which areas to pursue or develop.

Turn the page to begin reading about five kinds of student leadership.

1. Peer Ministry, or Peer Helping

Teenagers turn to their friends first when they have a problem. That's why Sarah has trained some of her high schoolers for peer ministry, and it's creating ministry moments that have strengthened the sense of community and caring she's building in her youth group. Peer ministry happens when you train and equip teenagers to care and listen to their friends. This develops student leaders who are offering their leadership in a peer ministry role. The benefits are certainly significant for the helpers as their skills, self-awareness, and ministry awareness grow.

Leader TALK

The value of peer ministry

" Peer ministry has been a crucial and rewarding building block to our youth ministry. Two years ago, I encouraged a lay person to be trained in peer ministry so she could teach it to our senior high youth. We had 10 students who enrolled in the training with her as their mentor, and we saw many wonderful things happen in this group throughout their year together. They were taught skills in befriending someone, making conversation, decision-making, faith issues, dealing with authority figures, and many other topics. It also helped some of the students with their own personal struggles. After the 14-week curriculum was completed, they asked me to keep meeting weekly. So we studied more teen issues such as dealing with suicide, anorexia, depression, and so on.

The young people in this group have been using their skills in many ways. Some have been involved with the peer mediator groups in their high schools. Others work with a university extension program where they perform dramas about teen issues. Others have assisted with retreats, middle school programs, and training a new group of peer ministers this year. They're active in their peer groups at school, supporting and listening to one another.

Teens seem to seek out others their own age to share about their problems, so this type of ministry is a benefit for the peer minister and for the friend being ministered to. Peer ministers do not always have the answers, but they're trained to think through the issues and refer someone to better help if necessary.

I've been delighted with these initial stages of senior high leadership. We have 10 trained peer ministers who are currently training six more. The possibilities for youth leadership after this training are limitless. It gives them permission to be themselves, use their best gifts, discover hidden talents, and ponder their relationship with God. "

—Heather Hultgren,
Our Savior Lutheran Church, Hastings, Minnesota

YOUTH Talk

How peer ministry has helped me

" Peer ministry has helped me see another person's point of view from a different angle. It helps me get along with other people by understanding what they're saying and feeling. It has made my faith grow and helped me understand what God wants to do in my life. It has helped me help other people when they're feeling low or down. "

—Travis Blomquist, sophomore, Hastings, Minnesota

" Peer ministry has helped me get closer to my friends and to God and to get more involved with the church. I believe in things more now than I did before. I try and have time by myself to pray or go pray with others during the prayer times we have at the church. Peer ministry has helped me think issues all the way through and not just from my point of view. It has helped me learn to listen and not talk as much. I am more open to God and some of the stuff that is going on in my life. "

—Katie Rowan, freshman, Hastings, Minnesota

2. Peer Evangelism

Peer evangelism develops student leaders who use their leadership roles within their natural friendship circles to share their faith in Christ with those friends. This group focuses on peer opportunities for evangelism and typically develops prayer support, campus clubs, encouragement and training opportunities, and accountability groups.

These student leaders are equipped to share their faith and desire to use the youth ministry programs as tools to help them present the gospel to their friends. These students are taught about evangelism, but, more importantly, they're held accountable to actually share their faith with their peers. A key verse for this area of leadership training comes from Philemon 6: "I pray that you may be active in sharing your faith."

A focus on peer evangelism has changed Casey's youth ministry. It has empowered students, increased prayer times, and given Casey a way to talk about the importance of evangelism in a new, strategic way. It has forced a change in some of the youth ministry programming and has challenged the adult leaders, but Casey would never go back to the old way.

If this is an interest area of yours, see **The Search for Peer Evangelism Excellence** (page 17) for some interesting data from a recent study on peer evangelism.

How students have impacted the ministry through peer evangelism

Three guys attended DC '97 (a Youth for Christ national conference) before they entered their junior year at Huntington North High School. Through the ministry of Campus Life, these guys have seen seven of their friends come to know Christ. They have used club settings, trips, and small groups to reach their friends. Peer evangelism works when students see their roles as being active in school communities as well as in their churches.

—Kent Yost,
Ft. Wayne, Ind., Youth for Christ

YOUTH Talk

Things I'm learning about sharing my faith

" Telling my non-Christian friends about my relationship with Jesus isn't always easy. In fact, it's hardly ever easy (although the more I do it, the easier it becomes). I get discouraged a lot—especially when I can't see God working and sometimes wonder if I'm doing something wrong. Since I'm learning a lot about the power of prayer and what it really means to give everything up to God and just trust, I believe that effectively sharing our faith requires three things:

• A lethal potion of prayer, unity, and unselfish love toward our non-Christian friends. With these ingredients our youth group is making a huge difference, but we're learning this is not an instantaneous event. In fact, it often is a long, tedious process, but it's soooo worth it!

• A committed adult leader. Student leaders need encouragement like we need fresh air. But it has to come from someone who's been through it before and has fought in these same battles—and won! It has to come from someone who has a passion for reaching the lost and whose fire is contagious. This essential encouragement can come from parents and peers, but it should also come from our youth pastors, since many of us don't come from Christian homes and our friends don't always have the essential experience needed to deal with all the setbacks we face.

• Effective outreach events. We need to have designated youth group times when we can feel safe about bringing our non-Christian friends. For example, Wednesday night meetings at my church are purely evangelistic and Sunday mornings are more to help us Christians grow spiritually. Everyone in my youth group knows that it's safe to bring our non-Christian friends on Wednesday nights because we know there will, in some way, be a salvation message that they will be able to understand without having any church background.

I used to be afraid to bring my friends to church sometimes, especially if I didn't know what the topic would be. I didn't want their first experience at my youth group to be one where a topic was discussed that they had no interest in or was totally irrelevant. I mean, what if we were going to talk about speaking in tongues or the chronologies found in Numbers, or something that my friends would have no clue about? Youth leaders need to be sensitive to that and consider their audience. The topic should be something that our non-Christian, unchurched friends can relate to.

If a youth group can be united in its effort to reach out, be friendly to the new teens who attend, and constantly support all their efforts with lots and lots of prayer, there is no limit to what they can accomplish through Christ. It's exciting to think about! "

—Kim Stumne,
sophomore, Crystal, Minnesota

3. Ministry Leadership Teams

This ministry area puts teenagers in specific ministry roles that often use a public forum, making it different from Servant Teams or other areas. This area usually calls for certain skills and often requires a great deal of time to practice and coordinate the ministry area. Ministry Leadership Teams usually involve groups of teenagers who are comfortable in up-front roles or doing public leadership. Examples are puppet teams, music teams that lead worship, small group leaders, and public evangelism teams.

YOUTH Talk

Lessons in leading worship

" Worship is a great thing. I can't think of anything I enjoy more than worshiping God. But leading worship can be a challenge for me. In the process of being a worship leader on our student-led worship team, God is teaching me about two major issues.

First, instead of worrying about leading worship, I need to focus on worshiping. If my heart is focused on worship, then others will be drawn into the worship experience.

Second, I'm learning how to be flexible in listening for God's voice. He wants to speak to us, but we have to learn to listen. There are many times when I'm leading worship that I realize that the focus really isn't on worship—for the students or for me. Lately God has been showing me how important it is to be aware of this and pray about it. I want to listen for his voice and be able to respond.

Worship is a great time to give God the opportunity to be God in our lives and let him display his great power and love to us. It's a great way to let our youth group focus on how good God is and unite in praising him. We need to give God the freedom to move. I'm thankful to be a part of the process. "

—Mark Schoolmeesters, junior, Plymouth, Minnesota

Calling kids to worship and prayer

From the parachurch perspective, it has been exciting to watch as worship and prayer have taken place when youth ministries network together. We have a worship and prayer service on the last Sunday of the month with music led by college students, times of testimony, Bible reading, and prayer led by high school students.

This year we've seen 75 to 150 students participate—it's been a great place for new Christians to come and begin worshiping God. I have never seen a better bridge from a parachurch ministry to the church, which is where we want them. The key—the body of Christ networking together.

—Kent Yost, Ft. Wayne, Ind., Youth for Christ

4. Servant Teams, or Work Teams

These teams address the need for certain tasks to be done, while at the same time they utilize the gifts and abilities of young people. This is where the youth ministry program creates intentional ministries where teenagers can serve the group with a wide variety of duties and responsibilities. Usually these roles are a behind-the-scenes kind of service and may involve physical responsibility. Examples are teams that create the bulletin boards or newsletters, run the sound system, and take photographs. **Servant Team Job Descriptions** (page 221) has sample job descriptions for Servant Teams.

5. Program Planning Leadership Team

This group is involved in the overall leadership of the youth ministry. This group of teenagers is involved in planning and decision-making for the entire youth ministry program. They work in partnership with the youth pastor to implement the youth ministry. There may be adults on this team, but it's designed to equip, train, and nurture the youth in leadership. This group meets on a regular basis to provide direct leadership over the youth ministry program.

Another team—often used, but not discussed in this book—involves youth participation on the existing adult leadership teams of the church. This simply means placing student representatives on the worship committee, church council, youth

The Search for Peer Evangelism Excellence

A survey conducted in 1997 by the Huntington College Link Institute studied the factors that contributed to effective peer evangelism. This two-year process included interviews, field site visits, and analysis of the extensive data. Here are some of the findings.

Survey participants
- 22 local youth ministries
- 424 student leaders were represented
- Meeting size of the youth ministries ranged from 35 to 350
- Student leader group size ranged from 6 to 51.

Student leader characteristics
Influences in becoming Christians
- 57.8% family member
- 17% outreach events or programs
- 4.3% friend

Leadership roles
- 42.9% encouraging others
- 15.9% up-front leadership
- 15.4% sharing their faith
- 13.2% inviting friends

Biggest obstacle in leading others to Christ
- 49% personal fears
- 33.8% busy schedules
- 10.6% lack of training

Person who helped the most to become active in sharing one's faith
- 22.5% youth pastor
- 17.1% Christian friends
- 14.6% personal experience
- 3.5% parents

Factor that helps the most in leading friends to Christ
- 25% other friends
- 21.3% trips and retreats
- 2.7% big conferences

Number of friends the student leader has helped become a Christian
- 12.9% no friends
- 65.6% 1 to 3 friends
- 17.9% 4 to 8 friends
- 3.6% 8 or more friends

Characteristics of evangelistically effective student leaders
- They see evangelism as a task, not a natural outgrowth of their relationship with Christ.
- They have relationships with non-Christians.
- They do not invest in programming efforts.
- They do not take leadership roles in running programs.
- They are focused on peer evangelism.

The role of mentor adults in peer evangelism
- They have a clear vision for peer evangelism:
  - ❖ They accept the responsibility to be models of faithful evangelism to their student leaders.
  - ❖ The adults are willing to yield responsibility to emerging student leaders who, because of the modeling dynamic, are more effective than the adults.
- They are available as sources of encouragement and training, and they provide structure.

Leader TALK

A volunteer's perspective on working with program planning leaders

" I worked with my youth pastor to train student leaders in a youth board setting. In the beginning, it was a tedious process. The teens were slow in developing a program and had to learn how to progress through a discussion and make decisions. I wanted to make the decisions for them, since I thought I had the experience to know the right answers. I had to learn to adjust how to do things because, in the end, our goal was to help the students become better leaders.

We had to help them experience the invaluable lessons of success and failure. Our job was to help them gain confidence in other responsibilities and grow as leaders. I saw students grow significantly and accomplish great things through their leadership. I also grew. I found I could be most helpful when I let them lead and do most of the talking.

My favorite times with student leaders were on our retreats. This is when barriers were torn down and real questions were asked and discussed. This is when the adult leaders gained credibility with the students. This is when we went beyond Sunday-only faith. These retreats can be one of the most valuable things you can do.

I count it a privilege to serve God alongside student leaders and believe it has helped keep me alive, vital, and continually challenged as an adult leader. Plus it has given me something to say on all those reference forms I have to fill out for jobs and colleges! "

—*Marg Tilleskjor,*
Lakeside Baptist Church, Duluth, Minnesota

- These adults develop programs to assist peer evangelism efforts:
  - ❖ They provide weekly accountability, individually or in small groups. Strong correlation between regular meetings with adults (not necessarily youth pastors) and peer evangelism activity.
  - ❖ They plan and direct quality programs that student leaders can depend on. The programs are distinctively Christian and are "safe" in the eyes of the students.
- These adults take advantage of events such as retreats and mission trips.
- They provide regular instruction from God's Word to help student leaders grow spiritually.

Peer evangelism is an essential ingredient to a healthy youth ministry. Evangelism does not just happen—it requires proactive thinking, planning, prayer, and programming. Adults must be intentional in creating opportunities for evangelism and developing support systems for teens.

—*Dave Rahn, Huntington College/Link Institute*
and Terry Linhart, Hope Missionary Church, Bluffton, Ind.

committee, or others. Some churches have used these committee representatives effectively, but they're rare. Students are often considered token members who are not trained or mentored in any way.

We encourage churches to have student representatives but to do so in addition to at least one of the five previously mentioned areas. To leave students to fend for themselves in adult settings without equipping, encouraging, or mentoring them does not develop them as leaders or create the relationships needed to support student leaders.

Leader TALK

Developing leaders

" What is a leader? The number of books on the topic is endless, but this simple acronym may get you started with your group.

Leaders are
L earners.

A teachable spirit is crucial. Leaders are always learning about themselves, their faith, and their leadership roles.

Leaders are
E ncouragers.

Look for those who have a spirit of encouragement. A person with a critical spirit may have power, but they will not be a true leader.

Leaders are
A ctive.

Leaders do something. They act. They live life. Leadership is not just theory or ideas. Help your students adopt the principle of active leadership and get them to consider the ways they're active as student leaders in the different areas of their lives.

Leaders have a
D eep faith in Christ.

Leaders are faithful disciples of Christ who want to be used by God. They have a solid faith that allows them to trust the Lord in all circumstances.

Leaders are
E xamples.

Like it or not, student leaders are examples to youth group members and school peers. They need to understand and accept this important role.

Leaders take
R isks.

Student leaders need to take risks in order to stand up for their faith in their schools. Leadership does not equate with popularity.

Leaders are
S ervants.

Be sure all your student leaders—especially those in public forms of leadership—are challenged to be servant leaders. Public leadership without the private attitude of service is empty and open to temptation. "

—*Tiger McLuen*

The Discipleship Foundation

The critical foundation in student leadership begins by addressing the internal issues of personal growth and discipleship. If we develop a student leadership program around skills alone, we will never have a complete impact. The external issues of leadership can often be learned, but the internal issues are the most vital because they're the glue that holds everything together.

No matter what you do or what skills you teach, it's crucial to remember that your primary task is to help ground your student leaders in their personal relationship with Christ. Being committed to following Jesus is the essential first ingredient in student leadership. Never assume that the discipleship component is being taken care of; it should be integrated into everything else you do to develop student leaders. If you forget that or assume it will just happen, your student leadership will eventually implode. The strength of leadership development is to stay anchored in the core issues of helping students mature in their faith. Let the leadership flow out of that focus, and your student leadership program is on its way.

Do One Thing Well

Student leadership is a plan to influence teenagers in specific ways that will strengthen their faith, develop their skills, and create ownership in the youth ministry program. If you and your youth ministry address the issue of student leadership, you can be more effective in reaching kids today. This generation of young people is looking for concrete ways to get involved. If you're serious about making a difference in a postmodern world, then involving young people in leadership is a critical component in youth ministry. As veteran youth worker Ray Johnston notes in *Developing Student Leaders,* "For eliminating youth worker burnout; turning around apathetic, uninvolved kids; and building long-term success in youth ministry, nothing equals a student leadership development program."

It's important to have a strategy to focus your efforts. You won't be able to develop student leaders in all five areas. Assess your circumstances and your ministry vision before choosing an area of concentration. Do one thing well and then expand.

Four Questions to Ask Yourself

Charting a new course requires counting the costs of such a venture. Developing student leaders will mean a challenge to your already busy schedule. It will mean shifting how you spend your time and how you get things done. The reality is that it's often harder to develop others and delegate responsibilities in the short run. If this means a change in how you do things, it's important to remember that change usually has a price. You need to be ready to do the hard work of following through on this idea. As you begin the journey of student leadership, be sure to consider your answers to these four key questions.

1 How does student leadership fit into my overall strategy for youth ministry?

Rick was energized by the seminar leader who attacked traditional youth programming. He identified with the struggle of creating programs that were poorly attended by apathetic young people. He felt this seminar would help turn things around at his church. He presented the challenge to his students at the next Wednesday night meeting and immediately changed his programming. He selected the student leaders and started to delegate responsibility in every area of the youth program.

After an initial burst of energy, Rick hit a brick wall of resistance and frustration from the student leaders, other young people, and a set of parents. The student leaders were frustrated and felt overextended. The other young people felt like the programs were poorly run, and the parents didn't understand what had happened to the youth group. At a special meeting Rick tried to defend his new ideas, but his arguments didn't convince the detractors. Rick's student leadership program was in serious trouble.

Rick made a common mistake in ministry. He saw student leadership as simply a new idea to be tried. In reality student leadership must be something important that the youth pastor has thought about and believes in. You must build a philosophy that includes adult and youth volunteers who will work together, and you must understand the rationale for incorporating student leadership training into your youth ministry vision. Teenagers are not to be a dumping ground for all the jobs that you and the adult volunteers don't want to do any longer. An effective student leadership program must be led by a youth leader who will commit to the philosophy, not use it as a quick fix. Then it can transform your ministry.

Parachurch ministry
Where to recruit student leaders for parachurch ministry

Through social and activity groups in the community
To get a diverse cross-section of Christian teens in your leadership, identify the social groups, clubs, teams, etc., in your schools and town—community theater, school bands and choirs, school and club sports teams, school speech team, Future Farmers of America, whatever. You're aiming for both males and females in a wide variety of interests. Next, identify the Christian students within these groups, and the Christians with noticeable commitment and leadership potential.

Through church youth groups
You'll often find student leaders for a parachurch ministry in strong church youth groups. So talk to local youth workers who can recommend student leader candidates for your parachurch ministry. Just keep the communication clear between you and churches, so no one gets the idea that your parachurch ministry isn't stealing kids from church youth groups. In fact, if you establish credibility and trust with your area churches, they just might appreciate the chance to send their student leaders to your training sessions.

Through your own cultivation
Growing your own may be the best way to "find" student leaders. Invest in students who have become Christians and been discipled through your ministry. These students usually are—
• Sold on the ministry.
• Loyal.
• Impacted by your ministry, with the desire to impact others.
• Understand the ministry strategy because they have experienced it.
• Understand the importance of multiplication.

And through recommendations from—
• Any adults who are aware of your ministry. They may know kids with the potential to become student leaders.
• Current student leaders who understand your mission. Give them opportunities to talk with other students and refer them to the ministry staff.
• Christian teachers and counselors.
• Middle youth workers and teachers, in order to target kids who were leaders in junior high.

—Mick Baker, Ft. Wayne, Ind., Youth for Christ

Your hard work should begin with a biblical basis for developing students in leadership. Two verses to begin with are found in 1 Timothy and in Jeremiah. 1 Timothy 4:12 says, "Don't let anyone look down on you because you are young, but set an example for the believers in speech, in life, in love, in faith and in purity." This challenge to Timothy is a call to teenagers and the church to understand the value and contributions of young people.

Another verse that speaks to this issue is Jeremiah 1:6-8. God called Jeremiah into leadership, and he gave an excuse, "Ah, Sovereign Lord...I do not know how to speak; I am only a child." God's answer is, "Do not say, 'I am only a child.' You must go to everyone I send you to and say whatever I command you. Do not be afraid of them, for I am with you and will rescue you."

As God used the young man Jeremiah, he can use young men and women today. You must believe that teens can be gifted by God (1 Corinthians 12:1-11) and that they can have a call (Ephesians 4:1-6, 11-13), just like adults.

The first step to making student leadership an effective part of your overall youth ministry is to integrate it into your vision and philosophy. If your church is small, then your first venture may be to develop a few students into program-planning leadership. Use this as a way to disciple them and give them a valued position alongside the adult leaders. Maybe your youth ministry vision is already outreach-oriented so developing peer evangelism and student-led worship and prayer teams would fit nicely. Build on your strong outreach focus and create specific student roles in your strategy. If your youth ministry is already strong on small groups, developing high school students as leaders of middle school small groups may be the place to start.

However you do this, it will be the silent efforts that will ensure the success of whatever follows. Without the background work, student leadership will be something you try for a while until the next amazing youth ministry idea comes along.

A passionate sense of why student leadership is important and how it fits into your ministry vision is the necessary first step toward making a difference. The rest of this chapter will help you develop your thoughts.

> ## *Spend some quiet time with these questions...*
>
> - Why I am interested in this subject?
>
> - Do we have a clear youth ministry vision statement? If so, how does student leadership fit into this vision? If not, what would it take to have one developed?
>
> - What is the biblical foundation to support training students as leaders?
>
> - Which of the five ministry teams seem to fit best into our ministry circumstances?
>
> - What questions do I have as I begin the process of developing student leaders?

Why should I develop student leaders?

The youth leader who is interested in creating leadership opportunities for students needs to think through and be able to articulate the reasons for this ministry emphasis. Here are a few reasons to support the development of student leaders.

Student leadership increases the breadth of your ministry. More can be done with trained student leaders. Your ministry can increase the number of tasks completed. It will also explore new areas that may be left untouched if led only by you and a few other adults. Student leadership will not just fill existing job openings; it will increase and expand what your church can do.

Student leadership turns spectators into participants. Too many influences in the church today reinforce observing the faith rather than being fully involved. People tend to support what they create. The key to increased student involvement may be to increase student ownership of the program. As Ray Johnston says, "When we major in entertaining students, we will most likely produce spectators. If we take on the challenge of equipping students for leadership, we will produce servant leaders."

Student leadership is encouraging. Experience proves that when student leadership is integrated into your philosophy and program, it will be a source of encouragement, excitement, and motivation. Working with student leaders has been exciting for us. It energized us to be with students who wanted to make a difference for Christ and whose faith was vital and alive. They were not perfect, but they became an important core group for us. We are convinced that it can be true for you as well.

A stretched faith is a growing faith. Leadership changes people. Doing the job of service and leadership affects people in a powerful way, and yet youth ministries don't often take advantage of this reality. Youths and adults learn best when they can put information into action. Their faith grows as they get stretched and challenged. They begin to believe it—not because the church said it was the right answer, but because they're experiencing God's spirit through serving. It's the call of the gospel to "not merely listen to the word, and so deceive yourselves. Do what it says." (James 1:22)

If you are serious about affecting lives, then you need to create ways for young people to be stretched and challenged. One way to do that is to develop an effective student leadership program. It's not the only way—certainly mission projects, service projects, volunteer opportunities, and others do this as well—but student leadership has powerful, long-term implications. This generation is looking for opportunities to *experience* their faith, not just hear another good devotional *about* their faith. If you are serious about stretching them and helping them to develop a personal faith that will last beyond your few years of influence, then student leadership should become a top priority.

Young people want to hear from their peers. Dawn got up to share the devotional for the meeting. She was a bit nervous and shifted her feet throughout her talk. She didn't have a three-point talk, wasn't very funny, and looked at her notes too often. It was short and to the point—even a bit blunt. In spite of all this, her youth worker found that Dawn's peers had loved the devotional. They had listened to her call to believe in Jesus. They wanted more devotionals from other students.

Adult egos often say that the adults need to do many of the leadership tasks so they can be assured of quality, content, and theology. But the truth is that kids are crying out for examples of how God is impacting their peers. Teenagers expect adults to sound spiritual, but they believe it when their friends declare God's truth

---

Leader TALK

The lesson from Bryan

" When Bryan first started coming to youth group, I was afraid he wouldn't stick around too long. True, his family had been involved with the church from practically the beginning, but Bryan just wasn't connecting with our youth group. He was very shy and introverted and hardly ever talked to anyone. I wondered how I could get into his head and see what made him tick. I wanted to try and plug him in somewhere so he would feel like he was part of our group, but I know that being around other students made him feel very uncomfortable.

Then one day I saw Bryan with a camera at another church event. He was taking photographs of everything imaginable. I seized the opportunity to ask him what he was doing. Bryan told me that he loved taking pictures and someone had asked him to snap a few shots that day and assemble them into an album. I asked him if he would consider doing the same thing at a few upcoming youth group events. Bryan was quick to respond with a very excited, "Yes! I would love to help!"

Now it's hard for me to remember the old introverted Bryan when I see him standing on the stage at our youth concerts, snapping photographs of the crowd. Or when I see him approach new students in our group and ask them if he can take their picture for a spot in the newsletter he puts together. Bryan is also creating some artwork that will hang on our main stage as our theme verse every quarter.

This formerly shy kid was brought out of his shell when God helped me to discover Bryan's talents. Now whenever I need behind-the-scenes help, I know where to find the right man for the job.

Every kid has a hidden talent that God can use in some way within our youth groups. Where would we be if it weren't for the people in our ministries who do all the thankless jobs? Thank you, God, for Bryan! "
—*Dave Ambrose,*
Parma Heights Baptist Church, Ohio

---

and action. Tap into this truth and your effectiveness increases.

The genius of student leadership is that it builds on the natural energy of teenagers. Energy is a by-product of adolescence. If directed, this energy can be very positive in leadership. If you can help kids be energetic about following Christ and let them express it in various leadership situations, the atmosphere of your youth ministry will change significantly. It could be as simple as having a young person share their faith or tell how God has answered a prayer. It may be a song, a game, or an idea shared. No matter what, it has the potential to energize rather than bore your students.

YOUTH Talk

Watching him do amazing things

" Student leadership taught me how little I am capable of doing, but how much God can accomplish through me. I learned to see that it was God who brought about salvation, spiritual growth, or personal discoveries in our group. This attitude has spread throughout my life as I continue to listen to the discernment of the Holy Spirit. It affects my conversations, decisions, and responses to opportunities. It's only by him, through him, and in him that anything has ever been accomplished.

Leading a small group has helped bring about a transformation in my heart, in my character, and in my God-led decisions. I stepped out of high school more mature, more responsible, and far more godly than I would have been if I had not been involved in student leadership. Leading a small group also encouraged me to pay special attention to spiritual disciplines. I had to be prepared. I had to hit a standard in ministry that set me apart. The Bible talks about God's higher expectations for leaders that call for a greater way of living. These scriptural challenges helped me to improve as a person and assisted me in my spiritual growth.

Through all of my leading and growing up, the most important principle continues to endure in my heart. I am nothing, as he is everything. There is nothing I can do apart from him. As I continue to travel along the road of Christian ministry, I will follow this one simple lesson: Where he goes, I will follow; where he wants me, I will be used only through His strength and not my own. "

—Melissa Bree D'Alexander,
college sophomore, Waco, Texas

3 Have I thought of the inconspicuous but critical issues in student leadership?

Let's look at some areas that are often overlooked when you start thinking about training student leaders.

Know the difference between authority and responsibility. Not knowing the difference between authority and responsibility is a common mistake in developing student leaders. Responsibility is when the teenagers carry out the details of the program. They work in the kitchen, set tables, run the sound system with the CDs provided by the youth leaders, and volunteer to sing the selected song after dinner. Authority is sharing power with young people, when teenagers have the power to make decisions about the program, decide the song, or pick which CDs to play. If one is to develop student leaders, there will need to be opportunities for your kids to learn about both authority and responsibility.

Don't assume that just because kids are doing work they have been trained in the area of authority. Physical responsibility is a great place to start off your younger student leaders, and some will be stronger in these areas. However, the opportunity for teenagers to have authority—within certain parameters—is a great leadership-training tool. Most adults are uncomfortable with giving teenagers any real authority, so this issue should be discussed and clear parameters need to be set.

It's interesting that Jesus used both of these training areas with his disciples. Often he had them helping him by distributing the loaves and fishes, bringing people to him, and so forth. But other times he sent them out with the authority to represent him (see Luke 10:1-19).

If you talk to any effective coach, you will hear someone who understands this concept.

No coach can throw the game-winning touchdown pass. Coaches know that their job is to equip the young person with the skills needed to throw that pass and the authority to do it when needed. So just like in athletic events, teenagers need to be given both authority and responsibility in other areas of their lives. Student leadership training brings these two vital elements into their faith life and their church experience as well.

The chart below helps define the major categories of responsibility in developing student leaders. While allowing for authority in each of these categories, the level of leadership is different as you move from left to right. Certain students will work best in physical responsibility areas—and younger students should begin here. Physical responsibility is the primary focus of the Servant Teams (described on page 16). Up-front program and people responsibilities are essential components to student leadership and include the Peer Ministry, Peer Evangelism, and Ministry Leadership Teams (described on page 14-

Physical Responsibility	*Up-Front Program Responsibility*	*People Responsibility*
Set up	Lead games	Peer evangelism
Clean up	Share testimony	Peer ministry
Work the sound system	Assist in teaching	Small group ministry
Produce fliers	Lead worship	Disciple others
Help with newsletter	Create or participate in drama	Outreach team
Oversee bulletin board	Present a devotional	Visitor follow-up
Take pictures	Create or participate in a puppet program	Big-brother and big-sister
Display pictures		programs

16). The Program Planning Leadership Team (described on page 16) places student leaders into all three areas of this chart.

Be clear about the role of the adults in this process. A youth worker needs to think about the level of adult leader involvement in an effective youth ministry program. Not thinking through this issue has killed many attempts at student leadership. Too often the youth are given all the responsibilities or else they're never fully integrated into leadership. Student leadership shouldn't mean handing over the entire youth group, worship, evangelism, or counseling program to the teenagers. Student leadership also includes the positive and necessary involvement of adult leaders.

Adults who are working with student leaders often need to take on new roles as they mentor, disciple, and encourage these young people. They need to be comfortable in giving the students both responsibility and authority. The adult leaders need to be supportive of student leadership and committed to developing youth ownership and shared leadership. They will usually need to talk about expectations and control issues before a student leadership program can begin. Training helps clarify how to do this while avoiding falling into old patterns of power and control. Your job is to think about these roles before the student leadership program begins and then continues to progress under your adults-as-coaches mindset. Help your adult volunteers see how they can lead the student leaders, work alongside them, be role models, and keep them on track.

Create an environment geared to success. Failure is a great teacher, and all leaders will eventually learn from failure. However, the real key is an environment that creates an opportunity for success. This is where you and the adult leadership team can really help. Work on mentoring your student leaders and doing everything you can to ensure their success in leadership. Be sure they have the skills needed to do the jobs you're asking them to do. Develop them in their leadership, and provide positive models for them. It may mean extra time in preparation and encouragement, but ministry success breeds greater willingness to risk again.

The behind-the-scenes work you do to guide the student leaders to feel good about their leadership roles will strengthen their desire to serve and be used. Whether it's doing a devotional, leading music, sharing their faith, doing the newsletter, or being on a committee, it is crucial that you and the mentoring adults work hard to set up each student for success. Do this and you help ensure that the necessary inner resources will be in place when failure does occur.

Don't stop with information. Student leadership should go beyond information to specific, tangible opportunities for your students to explore, implement, and interact. Your leadership training should help them understand deeper lessons and equip them with how to do what you're asking them to do. Whether it's peer counseling, peer evangelism, ministry teams, servant teams, or program planning, your student leadership training must also be working on both the biblical and the practical elements of leadership. Don't assume that an affirmation of their beliefs will translate into a transformation of their behavior. Help them experience it.

Leader HINT

You and your leaders should keep asking, "Could a student do this?"

Lead in prayer	Play an instrument
Sing a song	Lead a small group
Share their faith	Serve others
Do a drama	Be a model
Offer an idea	Be involved in worship
Lead a game	Teach or assist during vacation Bible school
Present a devotional	Share their faith at school
Encourage others	Promote a program
Promote an event	Share their hope and vision for youth ministry
Teach a song	Teach or assist in a Sunday school class

Be positive. The atmosphere you build is essential to the success of student leadership. You and your adult leaders should be people of encouragement who affirm teens who are willing to take the risk of leadership. Love them, and your training will have an impact. The atmosphere of your leadership training should involve a high degree of motivation mixed with an appropriate amount of encouragement. Find the right mix and watch your kids start taking risks.

Teach them about spiritual gifts. The biblical understanding that God gifts each believer in a unique way is a powerful basis for anyone in leadership. Kids need to be taught this essential understanding of leadership and grace. Student leadership without an accurate understanding of spiritual gifts is incomplete and doesn't speak a core biblical truth to these leaders. The power of a young person who understands this principle cannot be overstated. Two of the following sessions will address this issue and help you teach this subject to your students.

Help them be practical in their application of leadership. Too often kids are challenged to change their schools, yet they overlook their locker partners. Student leadership should be realistic and include enough specifics so students know what you are asking them to do. Every student should understand that they have been put in a unique circle of influence. Your job is to teach them to look around their lives so they can see where God has positioned them. Empower them to work within that circle, even if they feel it's too small or insignificant. Challenge them to live out their faith first and foremost inside those places where they already have an influence. Be sure that your training is practical enough so the students can use it in their schools and relationships.

Be clear about what student leadership is *not*. Student leadership is not a popularity contest. It isn't handing over the ministry to teenagers without direction, vision, or training. It isn't turning to your youth group and simply asking, "Well, what do

Leader TALK

How to help kids learn how to share their faith verbally

" As a youth worker, I run across one idea after another about how to help kids share their faith verbally. There are all kinds of curricula and magazines available to give you as many three-step processes as you can handle. But the most effective method I've seen so far is for the youth workers to model it for their kids.

One idea is to take a kid out for a Coke after school and begin building a relationship with him. Start talking to him about spiritual things until he becomes more comfortable with the idea. Tell him your own story (testimony) about how Jesus is making a difference in your life right now. Then give the student an opportunity to tell you about how he met Jesus and what God is doing in his life.

Gradually you could even begin talking to your waiter and build a friendship with him. As the Lord leads, move the conversation toward spiritual things. Allow the student to see how easy it is to turn a conversation spiritual, without coming across as too pushy or overbearing.

Once your teen begins to see how comfortable you are and how non-threatening it can be to share your faith verbally, he may even begin to jump in on some of your conversations. As you begin to sense his willingness to become more involved in the conversation, you may even try asking him how he feels about an issue while you're talking with the waiter. You may see him become more verbal about his faith right in front of your eyes. The main thing to remember is not to push him into anything too quickly. Model a verbal faith for him initially, and then allow God to give him the confidence he needs to speak up for himself in his own time. "

—Dave Ambrose,
Parma Heights Baptist Church, Ohio

you want to do?" It isn't dumping all the unpopular jobs onto kids. It isn't a way for the church council to get the gutters cleaned. In order to stay focused, you need to remain clear about what student leadership is *not*.

Every kid

Now to each one the manifestation of the Spirit is given for the common good.
—1 Corinthians 12:7

God has given every believer at least one spiritual gift that he intends to use to build the Kingdom of God.

As a leader of a youth ministry, my job is to allow Jesus to train me so that I see the gifts given to each of my kids. Some of these gifts are obvious and some are covered by so much pain and confusion that they may be very difficult to see. I have to work to see the handprint of Jesus on some of my kids.

It's my job to develop the gifts given to each of my kids and prepare them to use their gifts in the ministry of the Kingdom of God. Some will become leaders and some will become laborers in the Kingdom. Every kid has huge potential for impact in ministry. The key for us is to help give them direction.

—Dan Jessup, Pikes Peak, Colo., Young Life

Leader TALK

Lessons from a veteran

"I have learned many things over my 32 years in youth ministry. Some lessons I would want to pass on to others include—

• Do not do anything for young people that they're capable of doing themselves.

• In developing student leaders we are passing on the baton to the next generation. In a race this can be the most difficult part.

• Show students why, then tell them how to do it. Expose them to the reasons for the ministry; and once they have the passion for it, then give them the ways to do it.

• Teach kids how to think independently.

• Too many times we give students answers to remember instead of problems to solve. We need to teach kids to question more answers, instead of answering more questions.

• I have found it's better to love all my kids and see the potential that exists in everyone. Each young person is unique, and we should celebrate their uniqueness. God is creative. My hardest task has been to help kids see themselves as being significant.

• Give student leaders encouragement. Be their cheerleader. Have a ministry of affirmation. One of the most important ministries you have is believing in your kids.

• Give sincere praise. Be specific and do it privately. Doing it publicly can be social suicide for a teenager. No one wants to be known as the teacher's pet or the brown noser.

• Continuous fault-finding makes a kid deaf to the youth worker. The only time Jesus rebuked his disciples was for lack of faith.

• We are not called to preach love but to show love. If you love your kids unconditionally, you will be a pied piper to them. They will respond to you like a plant does to sunlight.

• God uses available people. I have always been convinced that the kid who is sharp enough to get into trouble is probably creative enough to become significant. We need to communicate to kids that they're someone in whom we have confidence.

• Look for progress in kids, not perfection. "

— Les Christie,
youth ministry department chair, San Jose Christian College

4 In my specific situation, what are the roadblocks to developing student leaders?

No ministry idea is risk-free. The idea of developing student leaders may sound positive and most would agree with it, but it may also be met with some resistance. You need to anticipate some of the negative responses in order to avoid creating more problems along the way. The roadblocks you experience may be from students, parents, staff, or church board members. It's important to think this issue through and have a plan. Developing student leaders has a variety of risks, and a few of these are highlighted below.

Elitism. If you create leadership opportunities, there is the potential for an elitist mentality to develop. This can happen when other people feel like the student leaders are better than everyone else. It can develop among parents who see the extra time and attention student leaders may receive. And it can also develop from within the student leadership group. They can begin to believe that they're higher up on some invisible, spiritual ladder because they put in more time, are up front, or have a title next to their name. On the other hand they can begin to develop a martyr mentality in relation to the rest of the youth group. You may hear a little Elijah-whining as they declare, "I have been very zealous for the Lord God Almighty...I am the only one left, and now they are trying to kill me too" (1 Kings 19:10).

It's very likely that the youth pastor or director will need to be up front with the students and address these attitudes at some point in the training and mentoring. If you don't, this can become a cancer to your strategy.

Unrealistic expectations. Many student leadership programs begin to struggle because of unfair or unrealistic expectations. If your expectations are too high, you create an environment of discouragement and failure. You need to remember that you are not dealing with trained, experienced, and mature leaders. These are teenagers. They can act like kids now and then. You must know their context, their issues, and their lives. Call them to a bigger view of the world, but love them when they can only be normal adolescents.

At the same time that you need to battle expectations that are too high, there is also the problem of having expectations that are too low. This will also ensure failure. Teenagers will sniff out a leadership program that is nothing new or challenging. Leadership should demand and expect something from the teenagers. If it doesn't, it isn't really developing leaders. The job of the church is to live in this tension of expectations. You need to have a program that expects something from the teenagers but is realistic at the same time.

Students can become performance based. A third potential problem is that your student leaders can begin to believe, "I'm okay because of what I do." This performance orientation is a recurring ministry battle— for teenagers and adults. You need to address this issue with your student leaders as they live in the truth that they're saved by grace alone in order to do good works (Ephesians 2:8-9). The world of the teenager is very focused on affirmation tied solely to how one looks or performs. Student leadership in the church should not fall prey to this worldview.

Even well-meaning adults tend to be dishonest with students about leadership. Many young people in the church have a problem with their image of an effective leader. They too often think that being in leadership means their prayer life is great, they read the Bible every day (and get lots out of it!), and never make mistakes. They see you and other adults and may assume that's how it is with you.

Too often, people in the church talk God language but they aren't honest. And too often leadership training is only a vocabulary test where the students learn what to say and when. If you're going to be helpful to your student leaders, it'll start when you take the risk to be

Leader
TALK

Don't set the bar too high

" On a retreat I recently took with my student leaders to a local camp and conference center, I was reminded not to set my hopes too high for student leadership. I was excited, as usual, about the upcoming fall schedule. I couldn't wait to run some of my thoughts and intentions past my core group of student leaders.

Things seemed to be progressing nicely over the course of the weekend. The students were responding to my challenges and seemed very mature during the long brainstorming sessions. We were coming up with some tremendously creative ideas for reaching their friends with the awesome message of Christ's love and forgiveness. There were some deep times of personal introspection and worship happening as well. I remember challenging the students on the area of personal holiness. There were several students who ended up breaking down in tears and repenting before the Lord. There was no doubt that we were all on a spiritual mountaintop experience.

We finished our weekend of planning and strategizing right on schedule and in a united spirit. I was genuinely excited that we were headed in the right direction and couldn't wait to see how the decisions we made would impact our entire youth ministry.

We jumped into the church van to head home, and I was still on top of the world. I had set high expectations, and the team had met my challenge with an equally impressive and mature acceptance of their roles as leaders.

Then it happened. About halfway home I heard several of the students begin to argue with each other about how far was too far when it came to sex outside of marriage. A few of these same students, who only hours earlier were impressing me with their deep spiritual commitment, were now shattering my hopes and dreams with their conversation concerning their liberal views of what constitutes sexual immorality. For a short time, I thought I would have to break up a fistfight right there in the church van.

It just proved to me again that no matter how mature we like to think our students are at times, we've got to remember that they're still kids! They don't have all the experiences under their belts that we do. They don't have all of the information they need to make an informed decision all of the time. That's why they need us. No matter how high we raise the bar, no matter how spiritual we think our kids are—they're still kids. Let's allow them to enjoy being kids and take the pressure off by not expecting too much from them all the time. Let's celebrate their God-given gift of being a teenager right alongside them! "

— Dave Ambrose,
Parma Heights Baptist Church, Ohio

honest with them about leadership. Leadership is God's grace in action, and you should figure out ways to teach and model this for them. Ask yourself what you're modeling to your potential leaders—and whether you show them the truth.

The issue of being performance-driven is dealt with in the honesty of humble leadership. The Bible is wonderfully honest and refreshingly frank about men and women who were used by God but had a life that was less than perfect. Too many kids compare what they know of their life with the image of other leaders, and they always come up feeling inferior. If you are serious about developing student leaders who are motivated by leadership, it's crucial to incorporate honesty into the process so they can experience God's grace in the midst of the challenge. If there isn't an atmosphere of honesty, then your leaders will have private struggles and fall away from leadership with deep frustration and guilt.

Adults tend to make student leadership a quick fix. It simply isn't. This issue of student leadership, perhaps more than any other in youth ministry, pushes the youth worker to think long-term. You are investing and planting. Most churches (and youth workers) struggle with this because there is such pressure to crank up something that will make a huge, short-term impact. Student leadership may not transform your ministry and triple your attendance, but it will do more to significantly impact the lives of your teenagers than just about anything else out there. Be sure you're okay with this before you begin and that you don't oversell the student leadership program to your committee.

Levels of LEADERSHIP

In an attempt to be honest about leadership, it's important to think through the process of developing another person.

These levels have no timeline to them, but they may get you thinking about how to mentor a student leader:

Level 1: I do, you watch—*observed leadership*
Level 2: I do, you do—*shared leadership*
Level 3: You do, I watch—*trained leadership*
Level 4: You do, I go do something else—*owned leadership*
Level 5: You do and develop someone else—*multiplied leadership*

Don't expect every leader to be at Level 4 or 5, and be sure that through this process your students get to know at least one adult leader well. Otherwise you remove students from the human dimension of leadership and just dump jobs on them without mentoring.

Implementing the Strategy

We have written this book not simply to be a list of theories or ideas about student leadership. Our desire is that you will actually implement steps to build a leadership team among your students. Consider these steps as you move ahead to the practical elements of implementation.

Seek God's direction. The first step to implementing any plan is to ask God for direction and then wonder about the possibilities. Your job will be to evaluate both your specific ministry context and the particular kids God has given to you. No youth group exists in a vacuum and you must adapt your thoughts to your particular situation. The first step in developing your plan is to assess where your young people are spiritually and build from this point. Use the questions in the **Assessing Our Student Leadership Potential** box (below) as a way to discuss the issue with key adult leaders.

When you begin this process, you need to be honest but also look for the possibilities. A good youth worker needs to have the courage to be honest but have "sanctified imagination" as well. Pray for discernment and wisdom as you assess your students and ministry so you can sense God's direction. Pray alone. Gather caring adults to wonder with you and pray together. Pray with some teenagers. Always pray before you rush into implementation.

Discern the opportunities. Here is where you have to decide which student leadership opportunities you will present to your group. This requires an honest assessment as already mentioned, and a willingness to make the opportunities work.

No matter what you decide, there should be adult leaders in place who are also excited about this new opportunity to develop student leaders. In other words, if you decide to start a student worship team because your ministry would benefit and there are teenagers who could develop in that area, then it's essential that you have one to three adults who are also excited about a student worship team and sense God's direction in this area. Otherwise, it will fall back on you to manage, direct, implement, and maintain it. Peer ministry? Do you have—or can you find—some adults who are willing to work in this area? Don't move ahead without lining up some help from adult leadership.

Do the hard work of sowing seeds. Before you rush out and change your ministry focus, it's crucial for you to sow the proper seeds to ensure long-term success. With any new idea, the wise leader has to do hard, behind-the-scenes work before a public announcement about a program is made. It would be important to have a clear, succinct statement of your vision and goals so you can articulate these to key church leaders.

Each church is different, but you will need to sow the idea with the pastor, the youth ministry committee, some of your students, and key adult leaders and parents in order to get a sense of support for this vision. This way you'll understand the questions and potential concerns that may arise as you implement your plan, which will help you build the necessary foundation for change. If you can answer their fears and present a clear

Assessing our student leadership potential

1. Which of the five student leadership areas fit our ministry vision and setting?

2. Identify the strengths, talents, and interests that exist in our adult leadership team.

3. What levels of spiritual maturity do we have in our group?

4. What are we already doing that could use student leadership and benefit from it?

5. Identify some of the talents, gifts, and interests that exist in our students.

rationale for the benefits, you will be able to move ahead with key support systems in place.

Remember—change is never neutral. There is a cost to change. A leader needs to have planted the right seeds in order to make the idea for change a reality that actually transforms things. If you do what you've always done, then you'll get what you've always had.

Build a motivational environment. When you present this concept to your students, an important aspect is the atmosphere that surrounds it. Your job is to build an atmosphere that believes young people can do incredible things and then calls them to the opportunities. There are many places where kids are challenged and motivated, but often the church is not one of those.

Why is it that the school can expect time, talent, and sacrifice from teens who want to be in a play or on a team, sing in the choir, play an instrument, work on the yearbook, or help in the office, but often the church doesn't? Work at motivating your students to see the potential in the student leadership program. Be practical. It may mean a young person needs to come in early every week or attend a monthly training session or meet monthly with an accountability group.

Set the standards. An important, and often overlooked, area of student leadership is in the area of standards. Of course Christians understand the need for grace, but it's imperative to set standards and expectations for your student leaders. Don't lower the bar of expectations or you will water down the whole idea of leadership. A simple truth is that leadership is not for everyone.

Remember—how you get them is how you keep them. Setting clear expectations and standards is crucial for the success of developing student leaders. To get you thinking about how you will articulate your leadership expectations, see **Student Leadership Expectations** (page 218) for samples of job descriptions and the student leadership commitment sheet.

Select the leaders. The development of student leaders begins with asking two questions, "How do we decide who are the student leaders?" and "How do we select them?" There are a variety of different ideas on how to select the leadership group, but the two most common methods are to have students elect them or adults choose them.

Students Elect. It has a democratic feel to it but runs the risk of only electing the popular teenagers. These teens may have high social status, but not a high level of spiritual commitment or interest in the youth ministry program. Election can also produce jealousy, contention, and division in a youth group. This kind of leader becomes more of a hindrance than an asset.

Creating a motivational environment

There is a dangerous attitude brewing in our culture around the issue of self-esteem and correction.

I have seen it with my children—their teachers are more concerned about encouraging my sons than instructing them.

This translates into an environment where they're encouraged but rarely corrected. This is not a motivational environment. It becomes an environment where mediocrity is expected and encouragement means little.

Building a strong motivational environment takes foresight and planning. A strong motivational environment is one where—

- The vision is big.
- The expectations are clear.
- The teaching is biblical.
- The correction is gentle.
- The encouragement is appropriate.
- The fun is plentiful.

—Dan Jessup,
Pikes Peak, Colo.,
Young Life

Leader HINT

Reflect on these questions—

- What personal and spiritual traits or characteristics will I require?
- What qualities am I looking for in a potential student leader?
- What attendance requirements will I have for my leaders?
- What training do they need in order to begin? In order to remain in leadership?
- What behavioral expectations do I have for my student leaders?

Parachurch ministry
Screening candidates for student leadership

• Learn (or review) the basics about candidates for students leadership: family background, interests, circumstances of their becoming Christians, why they want to be student leaders.

• Share with them your vision for the ministry, for student leadership of it, and of their roles in leadership.

• To identify expectations and accountability, use a student contract—a written record of the specific expectations and accountability structure for your ministry. (The document can also serve as a job description for the student.) The contract's signatures—yours and the student's—demonstrate your commitment to the student leader, and the student leader's commitment to her responsibilities. Keep a copy, and give a copy to the student.

Let student leaders know that, if they find themselves struggling to uphold any element of the contract, they should talk to an adult staffer right away.

• Have your student-leadership team develop a biblical process for discipline. (If they create it, they'll own it.) Conduct year-end evaluations of all student leaders, which can be as simple as having them grade themselves on each area of the contract. If the evaluation is good (but don't expect perfection), have the students sign new contracts for the upcoming year.
  And don't forget to let your student leaders evaluate you. This increases their commitment and sense of ownership.

• If you hear about or observe actions that go against expected behavior, give your students the benefit of the doubt—don't jump to conclusions, but talk with them face-to-face and give them an opportunity to explain. And be forewarned: if students feel guilty for wrongdoing, it's natural for them to belittle your ministry or the student leadership team (likely the source of the guilt) and possibly to stop coming.
  —*Mick Baker, Ft. Wayne, Ind., Youth for Christ*

Adults Choose. This usually means you or you and the other adult leaders choose the strong spiritual leaders subjectively, but it almost always creates resentment by other students and cries of favoritism. The other problem with this method is that it doesn't uncover the desirable leadership traits of those students who might be less obvious choices for student leadership positions.

The Objective Process. It's important that the selection process be an honest start to your expectations and understandings of leadership. You should not lower the expectations so that leadership is defined as anyone in the youth group. Leadership involves more than attendance and good intentions.

Two things are important as you select leaders:

1. *Clearly state your intentions and goals for the student leadership program.* Articulate the areas of student leadership you believe will work in your ministry. Identify your vision for this ministry and work on articulating it to others. Be able to put it in writing and to give verbal answers to anticipated questions.

2. *Let the* **process** *be the form of selection.* The best selection process is an honest , objective statement of what is expected.

YOUTH Talk

The six Cs of student leadership

"After being a student leader in high school, I believe a student should have the six Cs to be considered for a student leadership role.

1. The most important is a *confirmation* of God's call into leadership. The student must be sure that God is calling them to this role.

2. The student must also have *convictions*. Leadership requires people with convictions. If students have no guidelines or boundaries, they're more likely to slip and fall into sin. By having biblical convictions, students become more disciplined and have something to abide in.

3. The student must demonstrate *commitment*. If the student cannot come to church regularly, maintain friendships, or show up at agreed-upon events or activities, caution must be taken if they're going to be responsible for spiritually feeding a group of students. Commitment must be a high priority no matter how spiritually fit the student may be to lead.

4. The student must be capable or *competent*. Students need to be mature. If the student is at the same maturity level as those she is leading, there won't be much growth. This doesn't mean they should be perfect; it just means they must be farther ahead on their spiritual journey.

5. The most important quality is a *craving* for God. There needs to be a burning passion to get to know Jesus Christ. If there is no craving or passion for God, the student is not ready for the responsibility of uplifting and encouraging another student's walk.

6. The student must *care*. I firmly believe that the best *small group leaders* are those with the gift of shepherding. If a student has no desire to shepherd others but still wants to lead, he should not be a *small group leader*."
  — *Melissa Bree D'Alexander, college sophomore, Waco, Texas*

Selection is everything.

Leaders always lead. The real question is—in what direction are they going? I have always wondered why Jesus picked the twelve disciples. What did he see in them? It certainly wasn't their unwavering faith in God! Nor was it their upstanding moral fiber. There was something else that he saw in their lives that confirmed they would become the foundation upon which he would build his church. I think he knew that each one of them, in their own way, was a leader of people.

I know many non-Christian kids who are great leaders. If we can introduce them to Jesus Christ they will make a huge impact on their schools and families. I also know a good number of nominal believers who lead kids toward Jesus on Sunday morning and away from him on Friday night. When I select a leader, I'm always running the risk of having that person lead others in a direction away from the Master. Selection is everything!

But the disciples' ability to lead wasn't enough. Initially Jesus gave them one—and only one—command, "Follow me!" Yes, good leaders must be as good at following as they are at leading!

Therefore, when I select a leader in my ministry, I want to know whom they are following and will they help lead others toward Jesus? If they're a passionate leader they will no doubt make passionate mistakes (thank God for the Apostle Peter!). Jesus handpicked his people because he saw their God-given gifts to lead people and their internal willingness to follow the Master.

—*Dan Jessup, Pikes Peak, Colo., Young Life*

When creating the opportunity for our program planning leadership team (we called it the youth board), we'd write a serious letter to every youth group member in grades eight through 12 regarding the youth board, its roles and responsibilities, and an invitation to consider being involved in this leadership opportunity. A job description and application were included.

It was clear that there were expectations attached to the student leadership roles, and they had to fill out this application and be interviewed. We still had the opportunity to recruit some teenagers who we believed had leadership potential, but they had to complete the application process in order to be on the student leadership team.

The clarity of the standards and the selection process are the keys to making this work. Clearly hold up the standards during this process so people know what they're committing to.

Some kind of application or commitment sheet is essential to the process. The length of this will depend upon the leadership role. A six-week involvement with the servant team will not require the same amount of effort or dedication as a year-long commitment to the worship team or youth council. Whatever method you use to select student leaders, it's essential to challenge the teens and set clear expectations. A sure formula for failure will be to leave leadership positions open to everybody with no expectations attached to them.

Leader TALK

Ideas for selecting a student leader

"Scripture doesn't give us a specific pattern for the selection of leaders. But one Biblical principle is clear—God's leaders are to be chosen primarily on the strength of their spiritual lives, not their natural abilities. This doesn't mean God promotes incompetence. Rather, God chooses to use and develop the abilities of those people who are living in obedience to him, those who are willing to be used by God.

Following are two methods that I have found to be helpful.

- Several weeks before youth group leaders are to be selected have the entire group commit the selection to a time of prayer. On the election day give each voter a printed list of your youth group members in alphabetical order. Review some of the characteristics of a man or woman of God as found in 1 Corinthians 13:4-8, Galatians 5:22-23, 1 Timothy 3:8-13, Titus 1:7-9, and 2 Peter 1:5-8. Then instruct voters to circle the names of the members they feel God wants to lead the youth group. They can circle as many or as few as they want.

- Offer a five-week, leadership-training course and make it open to anyone in the youth group who would like to be a leader of the group. The first week almost the entire youth group shows up because they think it will be a social event. The second week fewer kids show up because they realize this is not just fun and games. By the fifth week a small handful remains. You make these your student leaders. The youth group has weeded itself down to this small group of leaders."

—*Les Christie, youth ministry department chair, San Jose Christian College*

Parachurch ministry
When a student leader needs to be removed

Usually you can avoid the entire necessity of removing students from leadership by making small corrections along the way. Don't let fear of conflict keep you from correcting students—with truth and love—on an ongoing basis.

Yet despite the adage that says you can't fire a volunteer, the fact is you can—and at times you must. So what do you do when someone needs to step down from leadership? And how can you cause as little pain as possible, to all parties?

- Know exactly why the student needs to be removed. The more thorough your written expectations are for student leaders, the easier it is to identify when a student needs to step down from leadership.
- Confirm your evaluation with other leaders you respect in your ministry—other staffers, members of your board or ministry oversight committee, church youth workers or pastors you know and trust.
- Meet with your student leader. With massive doses of love, compassion, and hope, do all you can to help the student see why she should step down, for how long—and what it will take to return to a leadership position.
- Keep written notes of the meeting. Write down what you talked about, the reasons behind your "firing" the student, and the plan by which the student can return to leadership. Give a copy of your notes to the student.
- Keep praying for the student. Pray for your relationship with him, his walk with Jesus, and his spiritual growth.

—Dan Jessup, Pikes Peak, Colo., Young Life

Train and develop them. After you recruit and select your student leadership team, it's essential to develop them in their area of leadership. This crucial component to leadership development is why the next section of this book exists. We believe that your job is to teach, model, nurture, and develop these young people into leaders. It's not something that will happen overnight, but it is something that you must work toward.

Focus on formation. It's important to note that this training and development is more than just giving information. Pure information, even if it has a Bible verse attached to it, is only the first step. Your student leadership program is about the formation of these young people into men and women whose relationship to Christ shows up in servant leadership. Student leadership begins with and builds from solid, personal discipleship. Forget discipleship and you may as well forget leadership.

As you train and develop your student leaders, it's important to plan for classroom training, modeling, individual mentoring, crisis experiences, and on-the-job training.

Build community among your student leaders. One of the foundational issues in any leadership training, but especially with the teenage audience, is to work at building community within the group. The relational focus of the adolescent makes this imperative. Therefore, you must include group-building elements in every training session or meeting. Have fun along the way as you grow in grace, serve others, and encourage one another.

The sessions that follow can be used in a variety of formats to equip your student leaders. They attempt to cover information but also help strengthen the bond that is necessary in an effective student

Jesus and developing leaders

In his book *Training of the 12* (Kregel Publications, 1979) author A. B. Bruce suggests that the ministry of Christ shows how he gave a significant amount of time to training and developing his disciples. He highlights the following components in the training of Jesus:

Classroom training
Jesus did give his disciples information. He set his agenda with them, even though they often didn't get it. His teachings, stories, and the Sermon on the Mount show this dimension.

Observation training
This component is when his disciples walked and observed Jesus. They were close enough to Jesus to go beyond the information to see the person. Our student leaders will need to see models of leadership, so it's essential that you and your key adult leaders understand your roles with the students.

Individual training
You can see in the gospels that Jesus spent time with the disciples in settings other than large groups. There was the personal touch and individual time necessary in developing others.

Crisis training
Much of the growth in the disciples came through crisis moments. Whether it was a boat in a storm, feeding the 5,000, or facing a hostile crowd, the disciples grew in their understanding of leadership through each experience. Student leadership development has to create opportunities where a crisis occurs for the young person—if none occur naturally—so their faith is stretched by actual experience.

On-the-job training
Jesus Christ sent his disciples out to experience ministry first hand. He set up the experience and then debriefed with them afterward, but he provided on-the-job training. Your student leadership program will need to set up opportunities for students to practice their leadership skills outside of your presence.

leadership program. Each session includes **Team Building** and **Team Prayer** as tools to help you build this community.

Have a regular time to meet. Developing student leaders assumes that they have not yet arrived. They're in process. Therefore it's essential to create the expectation that your student leaders meet with you and any appropriate adults on a regular basis. That may be weekly or—at a minimum—monthly. This meeting is in addition to any practice times needed for certain areas like puppet teams, drama teams, or worship leaders.

What's Ahead

By using the sessions in this manual, you'll cover the key leadership development ingredients such as community building, prayer, encouragement, and spiritual input. In addition to these elements, it's important to include planning time and any specific training you may need to offer for the ministry area. And there are always housekeeping details and the specific needs of your student leadership team that need to be considered. With all of these elements your student leadership meetings will need to be at least 90 minutes long, so plan accordingly.

The second part of this book is designed to assist you in the important role of training, equipping, and developing leaders. These sessions were created for you to use in the areas in which you're already training. Other format samples you may want to use are included in the appendix section. See **Mini Prayer Retreat** on pages 225-226 and **Student Leader Overnighter** on page 224.

Our prayer is that you will be able to use this resource to reach your goals while developing solid student leaders. God bless.

Using small groups

When I first began developing student leaders in a parachurch setting, I tried to provide a Bible study as a means for consistent discipleship and development. However, I found it very difficult to keep students' enthusiasm high at 7:00 in the morning.

In parachurch organizations we sometimes have to do things a little differently. There aren't any traditional times for students in our organization to gather—no Wednesday evenings and Sundays. Since most students are not morning people, we have turned to small groups and encouraged students to be interactive. Since we only have 45 minutes to meet, we try to be very focused—and it's amazing what can be achieved in such a short time with God's direction!

Through five years of growth and trying to develop student leaders, I have found small groups to be the most successful. This year I've focused about 90 percent of our time on prayer. The main emphasis has been on learning about prayer and seeing firsthand that when we pray, God works! Our prayer time has focused on our community, friends, and family, along with those we want to reach.

God has given these students the courage to reach out in love, and we have seen growth and development because of the desire of these students to flesh out their faith and be intimate with their Lord. I believe what has really set these small groups apart from others is the simple fact that they happen in school—on the front lines.

—*Mike Steiner,*
Ft. Wayne, Ind., Youth for Christ

Parachurch ministry
When is a student leader too young?

Chronological age is no clue to a student's readiness for leadership. Some students are chronologically immature, yet very mature spiritually. Others have been believers for some time, but are still spiritually young. Part of spiritual maturity is dealing with leadership's typical prestige, visibility, and control—all of which can be heady to an adolescent.

So ask yourself a few questions that may help you sort what kids will be best for what leadership duties.

☑ **Is the student a new believer still on a "conversion high"?** If so, great! Allow that passion to lead her into a disciplined walk with Jesus that can withstand testing—but just don't give her too much leadership early in her journey. Give her time to gather experience and wisdom. Nothing like falling down and getting back up to mature one's faith.

☑ **Does the student want to lead or serve?** Jesus said that even the Son of Man did not come to be served, but to serve (Mark 10:45). So is the student willing to take a position that others might consider to be at the bottom of the leadership ladder, then gradually move his way up into more influential and visible positions?

☑ **Has she earned the right to be in leadership?** Has her faith and life stood the test of time? Not necessarily of decades—these are young people, after all. But you should know something of her spiritual journey of the past year or so. Is she qualified for a leadership role? Desire to lead isn't enough. Actions speak loudly about a student's qualifications as a leader.

—*Dan Jessup, Pikes Peak, Colo., Young Life*

31 meetings that train student leaders

[curriculum]

Becoming a Leader

The point
What a leader looks like, and Moses as the perfectly imperfect example.

The point, unwrapped
Your students will explore—
- The qualities God looks for in leaders
- The benefits of functioning as a team committed to God and in community with each other

Where in the Word
Exodus

Team Building *15 min.*

Birthday Lineup
Have your student leaders stand in a semicircle. Ask them to order themselves by birth date, beginning with January on one side and December on the other. The challenge is to do this by gestures and creative nonverbal communication. Don't allow students to speak or to write questions or information.

When they have completed the lineup, have them share their names one by one (if they don't know each other) and their birth dates. Rearrange if necessary. Ask some questions like these—

- **What were you thinking and feeling as you did this task without talking to each other?**

- **What did this activity require of you as a team?**

- **What can you learn from this activity that you can apply as we serve together in leadership?**

Me against the World
Use this activity if your group is younger or antsy. Take a strip of masking tape and divide your meeting room in half. While you're doing that, have your students crumple up newspaper sheets into wads. Have students place half of the wads on each side of the masking tape line.

Recruit one volunteer to stand on one side of the line, and have the rest of the students stand on the other side. Explain that the object of the game is for each team, whether it's a team of one person or of many, to get more paper wads on the other team's side of the line. Begin the game and let students play for one minute. If time allows play additional rounds, giving each student a chance to play against the rest of the leadership team.

Then have students form two teams of equal size, and play the game for one more minute.

You'll need...
- masking tape
- old newspapers

Session

1

Discuss questions like this with your team—

- **What was it like to be one person against the rest of the group?**

- **What was it like to have a team of people playing with you?**

- **How is this game like trying to lead a youth ministry alone? Like trying to lead a youth ministry as a team?**

Who Would You Follow?

You can start by saying something like—

> As you just saw, it was much easier to get those paper wads across the dividing line when you had a team of people to help you. In the same way it's easier to minister when we're working as a team. Since you're part of this ministry team you're a leader in the area of [mention the purpose of the group], so we want to understand the qualities that God looks for in a good leader.

You'll need—
- whiteboard and markers

Have your student leaders brainstorm leadership qualities they think of as you read the names in the list below. Substitute or add current popular and local personalities. Have a student record the qualities on a whiteboard.

✓ Michael Jordan	✓ Faculty sponsor of a school club
✓ Abe Lincoln	✓ Steve Irwin, crocodile hunter
✓ Madonna	✓ Bill Gates, Microsoft maven
✓ Homer Simpson	✓ Your school principal
✓ Mother Theresa	✓ Our minister or youth leader
✓ A coach	✓ Eileen Collins, space shuttle commander

- **Which of these people would you follow? Why?**

- **Which of these people wouldn't you follow? Why not?**

- **Of the leadership qualities we've listed on the board, which are the most important for a good leader to have? Why?**

- **Do you think God considers any of these people to be good leaders? If so which ones and why?**

Throughout this book

whiteboard and markers are listed for activities that require writing for the entire group's viewing. Of course you can also use an overhead projector, a flip chart, butcher paper taped on the wall, or whatever other resources are available.

> Some of these people may be good leaders by human standards, but God has much higher expectations for people who lead the body of Christ (our youth group).

- **What qualities do you think God looks for in a leader?**

- **Do you have any of them? Which ones?**

- **Do you think others on this team do? Who has which ones?**

Team Huddle *15 min.*

Crazy Eights

Say something like—

> As leaders, we each need to understand our own God-given leadership qualities. We also need to build our team by knowing more about each other, including each other's leadership qualities, so we can work together effectively.

Divide students into pairs, and hand out plain paper and pencils. For the next five minutes partners list up to eight ways they're alike and eight ways they're different. Students may not list obvious physical attributes such as having two hands or two eyes.

Then have each student leader write down four reasons why they want to be on the leadership team and four attributes they have that make them a good leader (refer students to the list they made in the previous activity). Have partners share with each other what they wrote.

At the end of five minutes, have student leaders share with the larger group what they learned about their partners.

You'll need—
- a sheet of paper for each student
- pencils

Team Study *15 min.*

Make a transition by saying something like the following to your team—

> We all have leadership qualities, but what kind of leader does God choose to use? We're going to look at the life of a person from the Bible who was an unlikely candidate to be used by God, yet God worked mightily through him to accomplish eternal purposes.

Divide your group into four teams, distribute pencils and the **Becoming a Leader** handout (pages 41-42). Assign each team a passage and then give them seven minutes to read it and answer the corresponding questions. Each team should report its findings to the rest of the group in a one-minute summary.

You'll need—
- Bibles
- copies of **Becoming a Leader** (pages 41-42)
- pencils

Talkback

After your leaders have finished their presentations, discuss these questions with them—

- **How was Moses a good leader?**

- **What can we learn from him so we can lead our youth ministry well?**

- **What traps did Moses fall into that we should avoid?**

- **How can we avoid those traps?**

- **In Exodus 18, Moses learned the importance of working with a team of leaders.**

- **How can we rely on each other as we lead our youth ministry?**

Summarize today's session by saying—

It's no surprise that Moses had ups and downs as a leader. Sometimes he was a hero and other times he was a zero, but God still used him to make an incredible difference. The bottom line was Moses loved the Lord with all his heart and obeyed him. He took risks for the Lord, and he learned that he couldn't lead by himself.

In the same way, to become the leaders God wants us to be, we need to take on the attitude of Moses, that no matter what the success or failure is, we will continue to love the Lord and serve him first.

Moses learned about the faithfulness of God, and that's what our team will learn this year as we go through this leadership training adventure together.

Team Prayer *5 min.*

Close in prayer by having students share what they're excited about, as well as fears and concerns about the year. End by committing the year to the Lord.

Becoming a Leader

In your team read this portion of the life of Moses, and be prepared to make a one-minute report to the entire group.

Exodus 2:11-15

1. What **leadership** qualities did Moses exhibit in this story?

2. Where did he go wrong? What did he do right?

3. Rate Moses as a leader *(mark the scale where you think appropriate, 1 being poor and 10 being great).*

1 bumper sticker for a Pinto ————————————————————— poster child for leadership **10**

Becoming a Leader

[Moses the wimp]

In your team read this portion of the life of Moses, and be prepared to make a one-minute report to the entire group.

Exodus 3:1-14, Exodus 4:1-13

1. What **leadership** qualities did Moses exhibit in this story?

2. What four excuses did Moses use to try to get out of the job?

3. Rate Moses as a leader *(mark the scale where you think appropriate, 1 being poor and 10 being great).*

1 bumper sticker for a Pinto ————————————————————— poster child for leadership **10**

Becoming a Leader

[Moses the hero]

In your team read this portion of the life of Moses, and be prepared to make a one-minute report to the entire group.

Exodus 14

1. What leadership qualities did Moses exhibit in this story?

2. What did he do well? What didn't he do well?

3. Rate Moses as a leader *(mark the scale where you think appropriate, 1 being poor and 10 being great).*

1 bumper sticker for a Pinto ———————————— poster child for leadership **10**

✂ -

Becoming a Leader

[Moses the micromanager]

In your team read this portion of the life of Moses, and be prepared to make a one-minute report to the entire group.

Exodus 18:13-27

1. What **leadership** qualities did Moses exhibit in this story?

2. What advice did he receive from his father-in-law?

3. What benefits did Moses see when he developed a leadership team instead of doing all the work himself?

4. Rate Moses as a leader (mark the scale where you think appropriate).

1 bumper sticker for a Pinto ———————————— poster child for leadership **10**

Who's Really in Control?

The point
Jesus needs to be more than your Savior—he needs to be your Lord, too.

The point, unwrapped
Your student leaders will explore what it means for Jesus to be Lord even in a typical, routine day—and dare to submit themselves to his lordship.

Where in the word
Matthew

Team Building *15 min.*

A Candle in the Darkness
Read this powerful story to your team and then reflect on the questions—

Several years ago in Timisoara, Romania, Laszlo Tokes became pastor of Timisoara's small Hungarian Reformed Church. Tokes preached the Gospel boldly, and within two years membership had swelled to five thousand.

But success can be dangerous in a Communist country. Authorities stationed police officers in front of the church on Sundays, cradling machine guns. They hired thugs to attack Pastor Tokes. They confiscated his ration book so he couldn't buy food or fuel. Finally, in December 1989, they decided to send him into exile.

But when police arrived to hustle Pastor Tokes away, they were stopped cold. Around the entrance of the church stood a wall of humanity. Members of other churches, Baptist, Adventist, Pentecostal, Orthodox, Catholic, had joined together to protest.

Though police tried to disperse the crowd, the people held their post all day and into the night. Then, just after midnight, a 19-year-old Baptist student named Daniel Gavra pulled out a packet of candles. He lit one and passed it to his neighbor.

When Tokes peered out the window, he was struck by the warm glow reflecting off hundreds of faces. That moment, he said later, was the "turning point in my life." His religious prejudices evaporated. Here were members of the body of Christ, completely disregarding denominational divisions, joining hands in his defense.

It was a moving testimony to Christian unity.

The crowd stayed all through the night and the next night. Finally police broke through. They bashed in the church door, bloodied Pastor Tokes' face, then paraded him and his wife through the crowd and out into the night.

But that was not the end.

No, the religious protest led, as it always does, to political protest. The people streamed to the city square and began a full-scale demonstration against the Communist government. Again Daniel passed out his candles.

First they had burned for Christian unity; now they burned for freedom.

This was more than the government could tolerate. They brought in troops and ordered them to open fire on the crowd. Hundreds were shot. Young Daniel felt a searing pain as his leg was blown off. But the people of Timisoara stood bravely against the barrage of bullets. And by their example they inspired the entire population of Romania. Within days the nation had risen up and the bloody dictator Ceausescu was gone.

For the first time in half a century, Romanians celebrated Christmas in freedom.

From *More Hot Illustrations for Youth Talks* by Wayne Rice, Youth Specialties, 1995.

Daniel celebrated in the hospital, where he was learning to walk with crutches. His pastor came to offer sympathy, but Daniel wasn't looking for sympathy.

"Pastor, I don't mind so much the loss of a leg," he said. "After all, it was I who lit the first candle."

That candle lit up an entire country.

Ask your team some follow-up questions—

- What did you feel as you listened to this story? What made you feel that way?

- What risks did Daniel and his fellow Romanian Christians take? What other choices could they have made?

- What choice would you have made if you had been in that situation? Why?

- What were the results of the risks the Romanian Christians took?

- What do you think motivated them to take those risks?

- Explain how a person can live for herself and for God at the same time.

- Can Jesus be someone's Savior without being his Lord? Why or why not?

Now you can say something like the following—

Today's session asks the question, "Who is really in control—God or us?" Every day Christians face decisions about who or what will control our lives. Our old self wants to be in the driver's seat, yet God wants us to turn control over to him. In the story we read, we discovered the difference it can make when we follow God's lead instead of our own, allowing him to be in control and use us.

Team Huddle *15 min.*

Finish the Sentence

Have students get into groups of three or so while you distribute **Who's Really in Control?** (pages 47-48). Ask them to come to an agreement about the best way to finish the sentence, "Making Jesus Lord of your life means—" Have each small group discuss "Finish the Sentence" among themselves, then after 10 minutes or so bring their responses and ideas to the larger group.

You'll need...

• copies of **Who's Really in Control?** (pages 47-48), for students to discuss only **"Finish the sentence"**

• pencils, if students want to jot down notes

Team Study *25 min.*

After this portion of the discussion, tell the following story—

As a young man living in the last part of the nineteenth century, D. L. Moody sold shoes in Chicago and wondered what he was going to do with his life.

Then he encountered Jesus Christ.

Moody traveled overseas preaching the gospel to thousands of people. While he was in England searching for God's guidance, he heard a man at a Bible study say, "The world has yet to see what God can do with one man wholly committed to him." Moody decided that he was going to try to be that man—to live his life totally for Christ. He went on to become one of the greatest evangelists who ever lived.

If we want to be effective as leaders, we must commit our lives to God—totally, regularly, and decisively. Today we're going to look at what it means to make Jesus our Lord and be totally committed to him.

You'll need...

• copies of **Who's Really in Control?** (pages 47-48) from the last activity

• pencils, if students want to jot down notes

Have the students return to their groups of three to discuss the section "**Look up these verses**" in **Who's Really in Control?**

Talkback

Let a representative from each group share the group's decision about the main teaching of the passages. After all of the reps have shared, say—

From these sayings of Jesus we can see that it's impossible for us to live for ourselves and for God at the same time. Even as student leaders, it's possible to shortchange God and focus only on ourselves. It's only by seeking Christ and his kingdom first that we can experience life to the fullest extent possible.

In one sense, we choose many times a day whether to live for Christ or to indulge ourselves. In another sense, there will be milestone moments in your life when that choice is particularly stark and perhaps even anguishing. Such moments are remembered for life, and they often profoundly direct one's life course. In 2 Corinthians 5:15 we are told that Christ died so that we would stop living for ourselves and start living for him. Living for Christ not only ensures you of a life that is fuller and more meaningful, but allows you to be the leader God intends for you to be.

Have students return to their small groups to discuss the questions in "**Get a little transparent.**" Have the team gather together, and invite groups to share their answers to the last question.

Team Prayer *10 min.*

End this session by praying as a team. Let students take turns randomly, sharing brief prayers. Pray that the members of the leadership team would let God control their lives and make him Lord. Also pray that your leadership team members can serve as examples of the joy Christ brings to people who let him have total control of their lives.

Who's Really in Control?

Finish the sentence

Making Jesus the Lord of your life means—

List three practical ways an individual's life will be different if Jesus is his or her Lord.

1.

2.

3.

Look up these verses...

and answer the questions.

Matthew 6:24 *(Jesus applies the principle specifically to money—but just stay with the two-masters idea for a minute without going down the money road.)*

1. Why does the Bible say person can't serve two masters?

2. What happens to the person who tries to do this?

3. What are some current examples you've seen of this?

Matthew 6:31-34

1. What is the result of seeking Christ and his kingdom first?

2. What are all these things that Jesus is talking about?

3. What does God know about us?

(continued)

From *Student Leadership Training Manual* by Dennis "Tiger" McLuen & Chuck Wysong. Permission to reproduce this page granted only for use in the buyer's own youth group. www.YouthSpecialties.com

47

4. How does this impact whether you give God control of your life?

Matthew 16:24-26

1. According to these verses, what do we have to do to follow Christ?

2. What do you think it means to deny yourself and take up your cross?

3. This passage talks about a person who tries to save her life. How would you describe such a person?

4. What does the Scripture say will happen to this person?

5. Why do you think this is true?

6. This passage also talks about a person who loses her life. How would you describe such a person?

7. What does the Scripture say will happen to this person?

8. Why do you think this is true?

Get a little transparent...

...about yourself, within your small group.

- In what ways are you allowing Jesus to be the Lord of your life?

- In what ways are you keeping some control for yourself?

- What holds you back from giving God control over all aspects of your life?

- What would it take for you to "lose your life" and give God control over the dimensions of your life that you're keeping from him?

- What might happen if you do this?

- What could God do in our youth ministry if every leader on our team chose daily to live fully for him?

Leading by Encouraging

The point
Student leaders can make their group a "Barnabas" by encouraging and loving all those within their sphere of influence.

The point, unwrapped
Barnabas was the nickname of a traveling ministry partner of Apostle Paul. It's no coincidence that Barnabas means son of encouragement—encouragement being exactly what was needed by those persecuted groups of early Christians, whom Paul (the teacher) and Barnabas (the encourager) visited around the fringes of the Mediterranean Sea. So becoming a Barnabas simply means deliberately practicing the art of encouragement.

Where in the word
Acts, Hebrews

Team Building *15 min.*

Affirmation Game
This exercise will add to your students' abilities to encourage others—and encourage them as well. Have everyone go to a section of the butcher paper on the wall and write their names vertically (acrostic-style). Then ask them to mingle around the room writing encouraging words that begin with the letters of each other's names so eventually the names look like this:

You'll need—
- butcher paper taped to the walls prior to students' arrival
- markers

Kind

Always there for her friends

Ready for fun

Interesting, in love with God

Nice

Ask your team—

- **How did you feel as you wrote encouraging words about others?**

- **How did you feel as you read the encouraging words others wrote about you?**

- **What things did you learn about yourself from this experience, both as an encourager and as the one being encouraged?**

Team Huddle *5 min.*

Ask your team questions such as these—

- **In our world today, do you think people hear more positive or more negative things about themselves? Explain your answer.**

- **It has been said that it takes 10 positive comments to make up for one negative thing a person hears said about themselves. Do you agree with that statement? Why or why not?**

- **If this is true, what does this say about the world's need for encouragement? About the need for encouragement felt by those who attend our youth ministry?**

- **How would you define the word encourage? (a Webster dictionary defines it as "to inspire with courage, to give spirit or hope, to spur on, to give help.")**

You'll need—

- copies of **Becoming a Barnabas** (pages 52-53)
- pencils
- Bibles
- whiteboard and markers

Team Study *35 min.*

Becoming a Barnabas

Transition with a statement like this—

Just as we all like to receive encouragement, so does everyone else. In our Bible reading we are going to be introduced to a man that was such an encouragement to the apostles that they called him Barnabas, which means son of encouragement.

Hand each student a copy of **Becoming a Barnabas** (pages 52-53) and a pencil. Have the kids divide into three teams and assign each team a passage and a set of questions on the handout to complete.

Talkback

After the teams finish the worksheet, bring everyone back together and allow each team to report their findings. Then discuss these questions—

- **How can encouraging—inspiring others with courage and hope—help our youth ministry this year?**

- **What might happen in our youth ministry if we set an example of encouraging others?**

- **What are some specific attitudes we can adopt to foster an encouraging atmosphere in our youth ministry?**

- **What are some specific actions we can take to foster an encouraging atmosphere in our youth ministry?**

On a whiteboard, brainstorm several ways your youth ministry can become a place of encouragement. See ideas in **Student Leader Toolbox** (page 54).

Team Prayer *5 min.*

Close in prayer by having your student leaders complete this thought: "One area of my life I would like to grow in this year is—"

Wrap up the prayer by asking that Jesus, the greatest encourager of all, would take center stage in each student's life.

BECOMING A BARNABAS

ACTS 4:32-37

1. How did the believers in the early church treat each other? (4:32-35)

2. What effect do you think this had on their fellowship?

3. Who was Barnabas? (4:36)

4. What did he do? (4:36-37)

5. How might his action have encouraged his fellow believers?

6. How can we copy Barnabas' example in our youth ministry and in the world?

ACTS 11:19-26

1. What was one of the results of Stephen's death? (11:19)

2. Who was the news about Christ being told to? (11:19-21)

3. How did the church at Jerusalem respond to the news that many people were turning to God? (11:22)

4. How did Barnabas encourage the believers at Antioch? (11:23)

(continued)

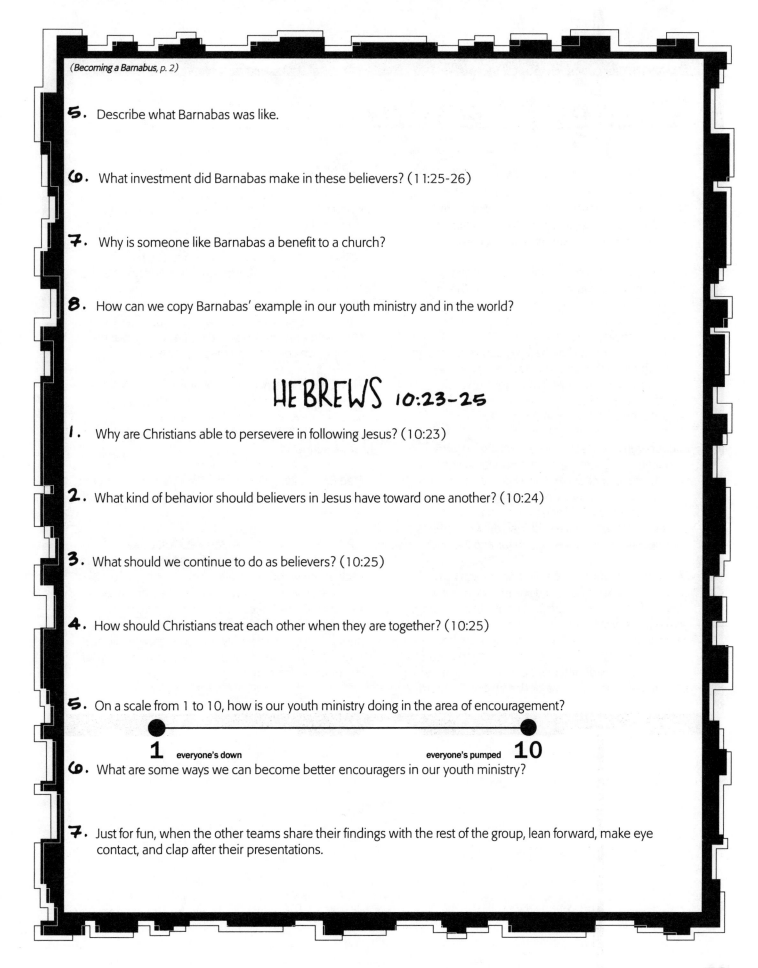

5. Describe what Barnabas was like.

6. What investment did Barnabas make in these believers? (11:25-26)

7. Why is someone like Barnabas a benefit to a church?

8. How can we copy Barnabas' example in our youth ministry and in the world?

HEBREWS 10:23-25

1. Why are Christians able to persevere in following Jesus? (10:23)

2. What kind of behavior should believers in Jesus have toward one another? (10:24)

3. What should we continue to do as believers? (10:25)

4. How should Christians treat each other when they are together? (10:25)

5. On a scale from 1 to 10, how is our youth ministry doing in the area of encouragement?

1 everyone's down   everyone's pumped **10**

6. What are some ways we can become better encouragers in our youth ministry?

7. Just for fun, when the other teams share their findings with the rest of the group, lean forward, make eye contact, and clap after their presentations.

Student Leader
TOOLBOX

ABCs of Youth Ministry. On a transparency write

LORD, OUR PRAYER IS THAT EVERY PERSON
WE COME IN CONTACT WITH WILL FEEL—

Then list the letters of the alphabet vertically. Brainstorm ways you'd like to see people in the youth ministry encouraged, one word or phrase for each letter of the alphabet. For example, *acceptance, belonging, cared for.*

When you're finished have student leaders sign their names on the transparency, then make paper copies to give to students. They can keep their copies in their Bibles or on their bulletin boards to remind them to be like Barnabas.

Encouragement Mission Statement. Brainstorm— then refine—a brief mission statement that reflects your desire to encourage everyone in the youth ministry. For example, "Every person matters to God. If all people matter to God, then they must matter to us. So we will strive to make each person who attends a youth event feel accepted, cared for, and included."

Doorknob Encouragement. Fill paper bags with candy, an affirming note, and some encouraging verses of Scripture. Decorate the outside of the bags with names of students and a colorful design. Cut out a hole in the top of the bags (just big enough to slip over a doorknob). Place them on the doorknobs of first-time visitors or other students who may need encouragement. The bags can be waiting for them when they come home from school or when they get up in the morning.

Locker Encouragement. Write encouraging notes and stuff them into friends' and new visitors' lockers.

Welcome Team. Stand near the door of the youth room and welcome new and regular attenders with chocolate kisses or hugs and express enthusiasm that they've come to the meeting or event.

The C.A.R.E. Team. (The Calling And Really Encouraging Team) Once every three months or so, call everyone on the phone for the sole purpose of offering encouragement and gathering prayer requests.

Free Baby-Sitting Date Night. Encourage your church families by providing free baby-sitting for a night out on the town.

T.P. Your Youth Group's Houses. (Total Prayer) Meet at the church for an all-night prayer meeting. Drive to each youth group member's house and spend 10 minutes praying for them, their families, and their growth in Christ. Leave a note on a piece of toilet paper that says, "You were T.P.'d last night. We totally prayed for you, your family, and your growth in Christ. Know that you are loved and accepted and that your life makes a difference."

Session 4

God Can Use Me?

The point
God can use you, imperfect as you are—no ifs, ands, or buts about it.

The point, unwrapped
Reluctant leaders have a bagful of excuses when God calls them to leadership positions. Yet God wants us to confide our doubts in him—and trust him that he trusts us as leaders.

Where in the word
Exodus, Judges, Isaiah, Jeremiah, Jonah, Luke

Team Building *10 min.*

Excuse Me!
For a little humor as you begin, read these excuses (which have circulated on the Internet for years) that were actually used to explain auto accidents:

> **I collided with a stationary truck coming the other way.**
> **A pedestrian hit me and went under my car.**
> **To avoid hitting the car in front of me, I struck the pedestrian.**
> **An invisible car came out of nowhere, struck my vehicle, and vanished.**
> **The indirect cause of this accident was a little guy in a small car with a big mouth.**
> **Coming home, I drove into the wrong house and collided with a tree I didn't have.**
> **In my attempt to hit a fly, I drove into a telephone pole.**
> **The guy was all over the road. I had to swerve a number of times before I hit him.**

Now you can say something like the following to your team—

> **Excusing one's own misbehavior is a national pastime. As Christian leaders, we're just as likely to rationalize our own unwillingness to live a Christian life as we are to follow God's call to lead others toward him.**

I Can't Because—
Give each student two index cards and a pencil. Instruct students to write on one card, **I'D LIKE TO—** and complete the sentence with something they'd like to do. Then have students write on the other card, **BUT I CAN'T, BECAUSE—** and complete the sentence. Inform students that their sentence completions can be serious or silly but not obscene or disrespectful.

   Collect the cards, keeping the two different kinds in separate piles, and shuffle each pile. Then draw the top card from each pile and read the **I'D LIKE TO—** and the **BUT I CAN'T, BECAUSE—** halves together. Continue this until you've read all the cards in both piles.

You'll need—
• index cards, two for each student
• pencils

4

Team Huddle

Transition by asking your team questions like these—

- **When do people tend to make excuses for their behavior?**

- **Why do people make excuses?**

- **What excuses do Christians make for living (or not living) out their faith in Christ?**

- **What excuses do Christian leaders make for not leading God's people when God calls them to do so?**

- **Answer this one silently to yourself: Have you ever made an excuse for not serving God when he has called you to lead? If so, why?**

Now you can say whatever gets the following point across to your team—

Leading others in Christ is a huge responsibility. Sometimes we don't feel up to the task. We think we're not spiritual enough, not perfect enough, and not talented enough. But God uses imperfect people to accomplish his tasks on earth.

Today we'll see how God used imperfect people to lead others. We'll see how these people, whom we now call giants of the faith, didn't feel adequate to do God's work and made excuses for not serving him. We'll see how God used them anyway, and we'll explore how God can use us too.

Verses	Excuse	God's response
Exodus 3:10-15	**Moses:** Who am I? I am not a great man. I don't know enough about God.	**God** promised to be with him.
Exodus 4:1-5	**Moses:** What if they don't listen to me or believe me?	**God** did a miracle by turning the staff into a snake.
Exodus 4:10-12	**Moses:** I am not eloquent. I am slow of speech. I am not talented enough to do the job.	**God** promised to help him speak and to teach him what to say.
Exodus 4:13-17	**Moses:** Please, send someone else.	**God** provided Aaron to help and promised to teach both of them what to say.
Judges 6:14-16	**Gideon:** My clan is the weakest, and I am the least in my family.	**God** promised to be with him.
Isaiah 6:1-7	**Isaiah:** I am a man of unclean lips. I am sinful.	**God** forgave him and removed his guilt.
Jeremiah 1:4-8	**Jeremiah:** I am only a child. I am too young for this job.	**God** promised to be with him and to rescue him.
Jonah 1:1-4; 2:1,7-3:1	**Jonah:** He ran away.	**God** pursued Jonah and kept calling him to obedience.
Luke 5:4-11	**Peter:** I am a sinful man.	**Jesus** ignored Peter's request to leave and instead called Peter to serve.

Team Study *20 min.*

Distribute pencils and **Uh, Sorry God, but I, uh, Really Can't Do This...** (page 58). Ask your student leaders to complete the chart by reading each passage, writing down the excuse the leader in that passage gave for not serving God, and then God's response to that excuse.

You may wish to have student leaders form groups, giving each group a few verses to look up. If you do this option, have groups present their findings but instruct the rest of the students to write on their handouts what each group found.

Here is what the completed chart should look like:

Talkback

When student leaders have completed their handouts, have them share their observations and ideas. The information in the chart above will help you add insights and clarify questions as needed.

As students share, emphasize the idea that even though these biblical people had lots of excuses, feeling unequal to the tasks God called them to perform, God continued to use them. In some cases God changed circumstances so their excuses no longer held, but in most cases he simply promised to be with these leaders in their weaknesses. Variations of this promise are found five times in these passages.

As you conclude, highlight the repeated nature of God's faithfulness by saying something like—

> **Do you notice how often the people had an excuse that explained why they shouldn't accept God's offer, but that excuse didn't seem to stop God? He keeps saying, "I'll be with you" and keeps pursuing people. If it's true for them, it's true for us!**

Have students jot down some of their own excuses at the bottom of the Excuses of a Leader handouts. When they've finished, invite them to share what they wrote. As they share, list their fears and concerns on the whiteboard.

When they've finished, write in big letters across the list—I WILL BE WITH YOU! Remind them of the basic promise that God has made.

Team Prayer *10 min.*

Have leaders get into small groups and begin to pray for each other regarding the fears and excuses listed on the board. Ask them to pray for boldness to be obedient and to recognize the faithfulness of God.

uh, sorry God, but i, uh, really can't do this...

[excuses of a leader]

Read the passages listed below. For each passage, write the excuse the leader gave for not serving God and God's response to the excuse.

Verses	Excuse	God's response
Exodus 3:10-15		
Exodus 4:1-5		
Exodus 4:10-12		
Exodus 4:13-17		
Judges 6:14-16		
Isaiah 6:1-7		
Jeremiah 1:4-8		
Jonah 1:1-4; 2:1, 7-3:1		
Luke 5:4-11		

My own excuses and fears

List your fears, concerns, worries, or excuses as they relate to being a student leader.

God's response is "I will be with you!"

From *Student Leadership Training Manual* by Dennis "Tiger" McLuen & Chuck Wysong. Permission to reproduce this page granted only for use in the buyer's own youth group. www.YouthSpecialties.com

The Self-Esteem of a Leader— Attitude Check

The point
Knowing your identity in Christ will help you lead and serve God's kingdom more effectively.

The point, unwrapped
Your student leaders will grasp the importance of knowing who they are in Christ.

Where in the word
Psalms, Jeremiah, John, Ephesians

Team Building *15 min.*

The F-Word Game
Tell your student leaders you are going to play The F-Word Game. Explain that you'll turn on the overhead projector for 10 seconds, and they should count all the Fs they see. The sentence that will be projected is, "The future of film is the result of scientific research and of experience." You'll find the master for the transparency on page 62.

After 10 seconds turn the projector off and ask for their answers. Most will say three or four. Some will say six, which is the correct answer, but don't disclose this information yet. Turn the overhead projector on again for 10 more seconds and then turn it off. Most of your kids will see all six Fs this time. If they don't, turn the overhead on one more time and tell them to look for all the ofs in the sentence.

Now ask your student leaders—

You'll need—
• transparency of the **F-Word Game** (page 62)

• overhead projector

- **What would happen if we took the of's out of the sentence?**

- **What does that tell you about the importance of a tiny word like of?**

- **How does this relate to your life and my life? (Many people today feel like an of. They feel insignificant, small, and unimportant. If that's you, the truth is that your life is important and it matters to God.)**

- **Do you ever feel like an of? If so, when?**

Session

5

You'll need—

- copies of **Winners and Losers** (page 63)
- pencils

You'll need—

- copies of **Who Are You?** (page 64)
- Bibles
- pencils
- a brand new music CD with the shrink wrap and price tag still on it
- an address label or sticker that's bigger than the price tag on the CD
- a red pen

Winners and Losers

Distribute pencils and copies of **Winners and Losers** (page 63), then divide your students into groups of three or four. Ask them to read the story, complete the questions as a small group, and then report their ideas back to the whole group.

Team Study

Have your student leaders stay in their teams and complete questions 1-6 of **Who Are You?** (page 64). When they've finished, ask your team—

Which of these verses are you most thankful for and why?

Share the following ideas with your team in your own words—

Many high school students believe three things are true about themselves: I'm ugly, I don't matter, and I don't fit in.

The reason they feel this way is that they judge themselves by a wrong set of values. They're confused about what gives them true and lasting worth as people. In our culture we tend to develop our self-concepts according to these four standards:

1. Things we own—possessions

2. Things we do—accomplishments

3. People we know—relationships

4. The way we look—physical appearance

- **Which of these standards do you tend to rely on to feel valuable? Why?**
- **What's the hazard of relying on these things for your self-worth?**
- **How can you avoid basing your self-image on these things?**

All of these standards influence how we feel about ourselves, but they don't reflect our real self-worth. In reality a healthy self-image is based on three facts that are true about each person. The main points are on your handout.

1. **You're unique.**
   - **You were created by the living, personal God and made in his image.**
   - **There's nobody else like you.**
   - **You can make a significant contribution.**

2. **You have intelligence.**

  • **You can think and make rational decisions.**

  • **You have the potential to learn, to change, and to create.**

3. **God loves you.**

  • **How can remembering these things boost our self-image in healthy ways?**

  • **Why is it sometimes hard to remember these things?**

  • **What can you do to remind yourself to base your self-worth on these truths?**

Hold up a brand new music CD and then pass it around the room for your students to examine (make sure you get it back). Now say something like—

How much do you think this CD is worth? (Whatever the price tag says.) So it's worth whatever amount of money I paid for it, right? Now pretend the value of this CD equals the death of Jesus Christ on your behalf.

Place a new price tag over the old one and use the red pen to write the words JESUS on it. Show the new price tag to the students.

That's the price God paid for you. So if we were to place price tags on ourselves, each one would read Jesus. You are worth Jesus to God because that is what he paid for you when Jesus died on the cross. The value, the price tag, that God has placed on your life is equal to how much he values his son Jesus. God says it this way in John 3:16, "For God so loved the world that he gave his one and only Son, that whoever believes in him shall not perish but have eternal life."

  How valuable do you feel now?

You'll need—
• supplies for the Lord's Supper

Team Prayer 20 min.

Close this session by serving the Lord's Supper. You might want to ask your pastor to come and participate in this meaningful time with your student leadership team. Focus on what Christ has done on your behalf. Emphasize the point of the last section—we are worth Jesus to God.

The future of film is the result of scientific research and of experience.

Tension Getter
Winners & Losers

Jason knows the reason no one ever talks to him—he's a loser. He's a dud in sports, his weight has always been a problem, and his acne makes him look like he has the chicken pox.

Terrel, one of the most popular guys at school, talks to Jason at church on Sunday, but on Monday morning, it's like Jason doesn't exist. When Jason and Terrel pass in the halls, Terrel ignores Jason—especially when Terrel's with his friends.

Terrel says it's tough being friends with Jason at school because a person can't be a winner if he talks to losers. Terrel doesn't want to risk his own acceptance with the other kids, so he won't risk being friends with Jason there.

1. Read between the lines here a little...besides what's stated obviously, what may be some other reasons Terrel treated Jason so poorly?

2. What does this tell you about how he feels about himself?

3. What would you do if you were in Terrel's shoes? Why?

4. What should you do? Why?

5. If Terrel were on our student leader team what advice would you give him?

6. Being a Christian changes some truths about ourselves. What are they? How can those truths help us be more effective in serving people like Jason?

Who Are You?

1. Circle three things people do to feel good about themselves.

Talk on the phone   Play sports   Dance   Go out on dates

Have lots of friends   Diet   Shop

Smoke   Drink alcohol   Serve   Bungee jump   Eat right

Spend money   Go to parties   Support an overseas child in poverty

Go to church   Go on vacation   Put other people down

2. Read Jeremiah 9:23. What should we not boast about?

3. Cross out the items in the above list that fit into the categories mentioned in Jeremiah 9:23.

4. Read Jeremiah 9:24. What should be the basis for our self-worth?

5. Box the items in the above list that fit these categories.

6. God loves us! Check out these verses and write down what God's love means for us.

Psalm 139:13-18   John 3:16-17   Ephesians 2:10

Jeremiah 31:3   John 8:32, 36

7. A healthy self-image is based on three facts, which are true about everyone:

     1. You are unique.   **2.** You have intelligence.   **3.** God loves you.

Which of these three is the most difficult for you to remember from day to day? Why?

What Pumps You Up?

The point
What pumps you up? Whatever it is, God has given it to you as a guide about how and where you should minister to others.

The point, unwrapped
God has placed in each of us a built-in magnet—call it a passion or motivation, if you want—that attracts us to people, functions, or causes where God wants us to minister.

Where in the word
Matthew

Team Building *15 min.*

Gotta Love Those Feelings
Instruct student leaders to form groups of four. Distribute copies of **Gotta Love Those Feelings** (page 67). Have students discuss their responses to the questions with each other, then gather your whole team back together and have several (or all) students share some of their groups' responses and insights. Then discuss a few questions like these—

- **Who or what tends to evoke strong feelings within you?**

- **How do you respond when you have a strong feeling about a person or a situation?**

- **Which feelings are most likely to motivate you to action? Why?**

Now say something like the following to transition into the next section—

At times we all have strong feelings about people or things in our lives. Feelings can lead us to make good decisions or bad decisions. Today we are going to discover how God has placed in each of us a divine motivation or passion designed to attract us to where he wants us to minister.

You'll need—
- copies of **Gotta Love Those Feelings** (page 67)
- pencils, if students want to jot down anything

Team Huddle *10 min.*

Distribute copies of **What Pumps You Up?** (page 68) to your students. In pairs, they should answer among themselves the first four questions. After five minutes or so, ask some (or all) pairs to share their responses with the entire group.

You'll need—
- copies of **What Pumps You Up?** (page 68)
- pencils

Session 6

Team Study *25 min.*

Then direct your students back to work, in pairs again, on the second part of **What Pumps You Up?**—the Bible study.

Talkback

Now gather the team together and ask each pair to share what they've written on the second half.

Share something like the following with your team—

Having a godly compassion or enthusiasm for something begins with sensing God's leading in a particular direction. People living in that leading and walking in that direction are fulfilling their God-given motivation and making a purposeful difference.

In Matthew 9:35-10:7 Jesus gives us what motivated him in a simple five-step strategy to reach and disciple our world.

• *Jesus went* through all the towns and villages. He went to be with the people. (9:35)

• *Jesus saw* the crowds and it caused him to feel a deep emotion for them. (9:36)

• *Jesus felt* or he had compassion or love from the gut. Why? Because they were harassed, helpless, and like sheep without a shepherd. (9:36)

• *Jesus prayed.* "Then he said to his disciples, 'The harvest is plentiful but the workers are few. Ask the Lord of the harvest, therefore, to send out workers into his harvest field.'" (9:37-38)

• *Jesus sent* the disciples, and they went and saw and felt and prayed—and the cycle continues today. (10:5)

For the next three weeks we're going to discover how God has uniquely designed each one of us for himself and for his purposes in this world.

Team Prayer *10 min.*

Pass out a **P.R.A.I.S.E. Card** (page 69) to each student leader. Challenge them to make a commitment to working through the points on the P.R.A.I.S.E. card over the next three weeks. They can start by praying every day. During the next several weeks, the group will be studying more in depth how God has placed motivation, spiritual gifts, and personality in each of them.

You'll need—

• P.R.A.I.S.E. cards (page 69), one for each student

Gotta Love
Those Feelings

Respond to these questions among your small group.

1. Something that really makes me nervous is—

2. I feel sad when—

3. I feel happiest when—

4. To me, the most frustrating thing is—

5. I'm bored whenever—

6. The feeling that most energizes and motivates me is—

Gotta Love
Those Feelings

Respond to these questions among your small group.

1. Something that really makes me nervous is—

2. I feel sad when—

3. I feel happiest when—

4. To me, the most frustrating thing is—

5. I'm bored whenever—

6. The feeling that most energizes and motivates me is—

What Pumps You Up?

List five things most high school students feel strongly about.

Why do you think high schoolers feel strongly about these?

List five things our student leadership team should feel strongly about.

Why should our student leadership team feel strongly about these?

Read Matthew 9:35-38, then respond to these:

1. Where did Jesus go? To do what? (9:35)

2. Where did Jesus preach and what did he preach? (9:35)

3. According to the passage, what emotion did Jesus feel when he saw the crowds of people arou
him? What do you think there was about the crowds that made Jesus feel that way?

4. What did Jesus' emotion compel him to do? (9:37-38).

5. How do you think Jesus would express this emotion, if he were here today speaking face-to-face with us
now, about our peers at school?

6. To what degree should *our* feelings be *Jesus'* feelings? Is this even possible? How hard
should we try (if at all) to generate Jesus' feelings?

7. When, if ever, did you feel about your friends or classmates *something* like what Jesus felt
about the crowds he saw?

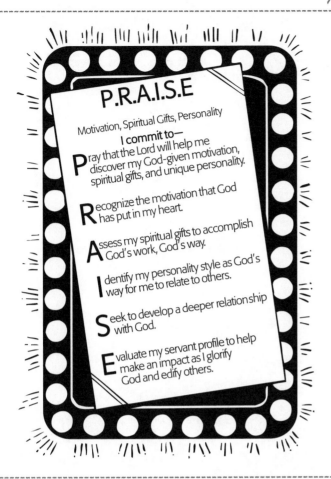

P.R.A.I.S.E

Motivation, Spiritual Gifts, Personality

I commit to—

Pray that the Lord will help me discover my God-given motivation, spiritual gifts, and unique personality.

Recognize the motivation that God has put in my heart.

Assess my spiritual gifts to accomplish God's work, God's way.

Identify my personality style as God's way for me to relate to others.

Seek to develop a deeper relationship with God.

Evaluate my servant profile to help make an impact as I glorify God and edify others.

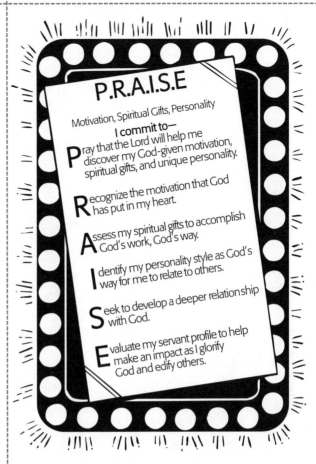

P.R.A.I.S.E

Motivation, Spiritual Gifts, Personality

I commit to—

Pray that the Lord will help me discover my God-given motivation, spiritual gifts, and unique personality.

Recognize the motivation that God has put in my heart.

Assess my spiritual gifts to accomplish God's work, God's way.

Identify my personality style as God's way for me to relate to others.

Seek to develop a deeper relationship with God.

Evaluate my servant profile to help make an impact as I glorify God and edify others.

P.R.A.I.S.E

Motivation, Spiritual Gifts, Personality

I commit to—

Pray that the Lord will help me discover my God-given motivation, spiritual gifts, and unique personality.

Recognize the motivation that God has put in my heart.

Assess my spiritual gifts to accomplish God's work, God's way.

Identify my personality style as God's way for me to relate to others.

Seek to develop a deeper relationship with God.

Evaluate my servant profile to help make an impact as I glorify God and edify others.

P.R.A.I.S.E

Motivation, Spiritual Gifts, Personality

I commit to—

Pray that the Lord will help me discover my God-given motivation, spiritual gifts, and unique personality.

Recognize the motivation that God has put in my heart.

Assess my spiritual gifts to accomplish God's work, God's way.

Identify my personality style as God's way for me to relate to others.

Seek to develop a deeper relationship with God.

Evaluate my servant profile to help make an impact as I glorify God and edify others.

Discover Your Spiritual Gifts

The point
God has given you something special—something he wants you to help build his kingdom with.

The point, unwrapped
Knowing and using their spiritual gifts help student leaders serve God and their church—not to mention help fulfill God's purposes for their own lives.

Where in the word
Matthew, Romans, 1 Corinthians, Ephesians, 1 Timothy, 1 Peter

Team Building *25 min.*

The Bodies
Read the following illustration out loud, and then discuss the questions.

> Once upon a time there were four people named Everybody, Somebody, Nobody, and Anybody.
>
> When there was an important job to be done, Everybody was sure that Somebody would do it. Anybody could have done it. But Nobody realized that Nobody would do it.
>
> So it ended up that Everybody blamed Somebody when Nobody did what Anybody could have done in the first place.

You'll need—
• about 1000 3x5 index cards

Now ask—

- **So what's the point of this little fable?**
- **What must happen for something to get done?**
- **What does this mean for getting things done in our own youth ministry?**

Card Castles
After your discussion, you can say to your team—

> Being in ministry is not a one-person show. Making an impact for Christ in and through our youth ministry will require each of us to use our gifts, personalities, and motivations. We need to work together to accomplish God's purpose for our church and our lives.

Divide students into clusters of 3 to 4, then explain that each cluster will create a structure from index cards. To do so they may fold the cards once—or stack them flat, one on top of another.

That's not all. Each group must connect its structure to other structures built by other groups. (If you have fewer than four groups, just have them each connect their structures to all the other structures in the room.) And—the groups must do this all without speaking.

The more cards and time your student leaders have, the more elaborate their structures and connections.

> If your group is on the small side, like 3 or 4 students, simply let them build the index-card structure together. Or put yourself in the mix to make at least two pairs, so you have the benefit of joining two card structures into one.

Ask your team—

- **How did you feel during this activity?**

- **What did it take to accomplish this activity?**

- **Could you have accomplished this by yourself? Why or why not? (Obviously you shouldn't ask this question if you had students working alone.)**

- **Did you find yourself or others serving specific roles as you accomplished this task? If so, what roles did people play?**

- **How is this activity like working together as a leadership team in our youth ministry?**

Team Huddle *5 min.*

Recruit one of your student leaders to read aloud 1 Corinthians 12:12-31. Ask your team—

- **How does this Bible passage relate to what you just did with the card castles?**

- **What does this passage tell us about how our team should work together?**

- **What does this passage tell us about each person on our leadership team?**

Share insights about spiritual gifts with your team in words something like this—

Each of us has been given different gifts to accomplish God's ministry on this earth. For us to become a youth ministry that makes an impact for God, we need to discover what spiritual gifts are and how to apply them to our lives and ministry.

Some people have great talents and abilities that tend to focus on the individual who possesses such talents. But spiritual gifts are given to all Christians when they make their life commitments to Christ.

By knowing your spiritual gifts and using them, you will be better able to know and accomplish God's will and purpose for your life.

Ask your team—

- **What do you think a spiritual gift is?**
- **Why should each of us on this team know everyone else's spiritual gifts?**
- **How do people discover their spiritual gifts?**

Team Study *20 min.*

You'll need—
- copies of **Discover Your Spiritual Gifts** (page 74)
- Bibles
- pencils

Pass out pencils and **Discover Your Spiritual Gifts** (page 74). Have your student leaders go through the handouts with their group members from the Card Castles activity.

After they've finished, gather your students back together and ask them to share what they discovered about spiritual gifts.

Team Prayer *10 min.*

Explain to your group—

God has given every believer in Jesus Christ at least one spiritual gift. Next week we are going to take a spiritual gifts test to help us discover and determine the gift or gifts that God has given each of us.

Close your time by asking God to give your team wisdom and direction about their individual spiritual gifts and how they might use them for his purposes in your church's youth ministry.

Discover Your Spiritual Gifts

A person who knows, loves, and trusts Jesus Christ belongs in God's family and is made alive by the Holy Spirit. Everyone who has God's Spirit has some spiritual gift or gifts for the sole purpose of accomplishing God's work.

1. Rewrite the above thought in your own words.

2. What does the Bible say about the need to know our spiritual gifts?

    Matthew 25:14-30

    1 Corinthians 12:1

    1 Timothy 4:14

3. Read 1 Corinthians 12:11. Who determines how the gifts are distributed?

4. Read 1 Peter 4:10-11. What are we supposed to do with our spiritual gifts?

5. List spiritual gifts mentioned in the following passages.

    Romans 12:4-8

    1 Corinthians 12:1-11, 27-28

    Ephesians 4:11-12

6. After reading these verses and thinking about these questions, what do you about how God wants to use you?

7. How can knowing our spiritual gifts help our student leadership team make an impact for Christ in our community?

Discover Your Spiritual Gifts, Part Deux

The point
God has given you something special, something he wants you to use to build his kingdom—part two.

The point, unwrapped
Leaders (student or otherwise) need to understand their place in the body of Christ by discovering their spiritual gifts—abilities and personality traits, given by God—that enable your students to serve God and the church.

Where in the word
Romans, Colossians

Team Building *10 min.*

The Secret Ingredients
Ask for six volunteers to help with an object lesson. As your volunteers come to the front, set out on a table the six Styrofoam cups each filled with a different ingredient and covered with a small piece of foil. Have the volunteers each stand behind one of the cups and close their eyes as you remove the foil. One at a time, have them dip a finger into the cup in front of them, taste the ingredient, and describe what they taste. Record their descriptions on a whiteboard.

After they're through describing the ingredients, say something like—

These six brave volunteers just touched and tasted six ingredients. Individually each ingredient has its own unique taste and purpose. But when we mix all six ingredients together, they work together to make cookies!

You'll need—
- six Styrofoam cups each containing one of the following ingredients: butter, salt, sugar, bittersweet chocolate, an egg, and flour
- aluminum foil
- whiteboard and markers
- box of chocolate cookies
- table

At this point hand out cookies to the entire group. Remind leaders that at the last meeting they explored the concept of spiritual gifts. Ask questions along these lines—

- **What did we learn about spiritual gifts at the last meeting?**
- **How are the individual ingredients in our activity like each of us possessing spiritual gifts? How are they different?**
- **How does the fact that these ingredients can mix to make cookies resemble how we all can mix together with our spiritual gifts to do God's will? How is it different?**

Session

8

Now you could say to your team—

A good chef understands the ingredients she uses in her cooking. She knows how sugar and baking soda and egg work—not just individually but together—and can use them to create delicious foods we enjoy. In the same way, God has given each of us a special gift and knows how we can work—not just individually but together—to minister to those around us.

We can trust God to put us together in effective ways, but it also helps us to know our own and each other's spiritual gifts so we can serve God and his church and accomplish his will for our lives.

You'll need—
• Bibles

Team Huddle *10 min.*

Ask your student leaders to turn in their Bibles to Romans 12:3-11 and read these verses together. You can ask your team questions like these—

- • How should Christians think about themselves? (12:3)

- • What did Paul, the writer of Romans, use the human body to illustrate? (12:4-5)

- • What does the statement in verse 3 mean in the context of being a part of Christ's body?

- • What are the gifts listed in 12:6-8?

  - • What other talents might be spiritual gifts?

  - • How should each person use their gifts? (12:6-8)

  - • How can knowing our individual gifts help our youth ministry make an even greater impact for Jesus Christ?

Leader Hint—

• If you have time and you feel your team is open to this, focus on one student leader at a time. Allow students to share what they think their spiritual gifts are. Allow the whole team to bombard students, one by one, with encouraging words to affirm their gifts or suggest others.

• Ask your student leaders to hand in their questionnaires for you to copy and place on file. Return the questionnaires the next week.

Team Study *25 min.*

Discover Your Spiritual Gifts

Distribute pencils and copies of **Discover Your Spiritual Gifts, Part Deux** (pages 78-79). Explain that the handout is a spiritual gifts questionnaire that will help your leaders discover how God has gifted them for ministry. Assure them that there are no right or wrong answers. Encourage them to take their time filling out the questionnaire and to answer each question honestly.

Before your student leaders begin, pray that God would show them how he has uniquely gifted them for ministry.

After they've completed the questionnaire, they should tabulate their scores according to the instructions, then read the Explanation and Assessment sections. Invite leaders to share what they've discovered about themselves. Don't force anyone to share, but give encouragement to those who do.

You'll need—
• copies of **Discover Your Spiritual Gifts, Part Deux** (pages 78-79)

• pencils

Team Prayer *15 min.*

Have leaders form pairs. Pray through Colossians 1:9-12 for each other by putting the partner's name into it. Here's a sample.

Lord today I ask that Miguel may be filled with the knowledge of your will through all wisdom and spiritual understanding. Help Miguel walk worthy of you Lord, fully pleasing to you and may Miguel be fruitful in every good work and increasing in knowledge of you. I pray that Miguel may be strengthened with your power might so that he will have endurance and patience.

Discover Your Spiritual Gifts, Part Deux

For each question, write the number of the stament that fits you best.

3 = That's me!   2 = This is probably me.   1 = This is probably not me.   0 = Definitely not me!

____ 1. I try to worry more about the needs of others than my own.

____ 2. People come to me when they need to talk about a problem.

____ 3. I would like to give money to those in need.

____ 4. I enjoy explaining the Bible to others.

____ 5. I like to try to help others know God better.

____ 6. I don't mind being seen with people who aren't that popular.

____ 7. When I see needy people on cold nights, I really feel like inviting them to my home.

____ 8. On Friday nights, I am usually the one who decides where we go and what we do.

____ 9. I like to tell others about my relationship with God.

____ 10. I have confidence that God will get me through both good and bad times.

____ 11. I like doing jobs that most other people don't want to do.

____ 12. I am known for my positive attitude.

____ 13. I get a real kick out of giving stuff away.

____ 14. I like studying the Bible so I can explain it to others.

____ 15. I like to pray for and with others.

____ 16. I would like to work with disabled people.

____ 17. I like having friends stay overnight at my house.

____ 18. I like to organize and motivate groups of people.

____ 19. I can sometimes direct conversations toward God in a comfortable way.

____ 20. I believe that God can do things that seem impossible.

____ 21. I have helped other people so their work was easier.

____ 22. I like to help sad people feel better.

____ 23. I try to be smart with my money so that I can give extra money to people who need it.

____ 24. I like learning and studying the Bible.

____ 25. I would love to lead a Bible study with my friends.

____ 26. I feel very sympathetic toward the needy.

____ 27. I don't feel disrupted when there are guests at my home.

____ 28. I have encouraged others to finish a project.

____ 29. I would like to help someone else become a Christian.

____ 30. I have confidence that God will keep his promises even when things are bad.

____ 31. I don't mind doing little jobs that other people don't consider important.

____ 32. I can encourage others through what I say.

____ 33. I know that God will meet my needs, so I want to give freely to others.

____ 34. I can show others what many verses in the Bible mean.

____ 35. I like to serve people to show that God cares for them.

____ 36. If a friend is sick, I call to see how they are doing.

____ 37. I like having company come to my house.

____ 38. I would like to lead, inspire, and motivate people to do God's work.

____ 39. I would like to tell others that Jesus is the Savior and help them see the positive results.

____ 40. I trust that I can call on God and know that he will be there when "impossible" situations happen.

____ 41. Sometimes when I do jobs, nobody notices, but I don't mind.

____ 42. I like it when people are happier after I have talked to them.

____ 43. I have given away some of my money or belongings to those in need.

____ 44. I think that I could show others how to find answers on their own.

____ 45. I would like to help bring people back to Christ who have wandered away from him.

____ 46. When I see a homeless person, I really want to help.

____ 47. My friends come over to my house because they feel comfortable there.

____ 48. When I'm in a group, sometimes people look to me to take charge.

____ 49. I take any opportunity I can to tell people about Christ.

____ 50. When everything looks bad, I can still trust God.

(continued)

Tabulation

Put the number (0 to 3) of your response to each test question in the next to the appropriate number below. Then, add up the numbers in each row (reading across) and record the total.

					TOTAL	GIFT
1 _____	11 _____	21 _____	31 _____	41 _____	_____	A _____
2 _____	12 _____	22 _____	32 _____	42 _____	_____	B _____
3 _____	13 _____	23 _____	33 _____	43 _____	_____	C _____
4 _____	14 _____	24 _____	34 _____	44 _____	_____	D _____
5 _____	15 _____	25 _____	35 _____	45 _____	_____	E _____
6 _____	16 _____	26 _____	36 _____	46 _____	_____	F _____
7 _____	17 _____	27 _____	37 _____	47 _____	_____	G _____
8 _____	18 _____	28 _____	38 _____	48 _____	_____	H _____
9 _____	19 _____	29 _____	39 _____	49 _____	_____	I _____
10 _____	20 _____	30 _____	40 _____	50 _____	_____	J _____

Explanation

Gift A: **Helping.** The ability to assist and serve other people.

Gift B: **Encouraging.** The ability to support people and to help them regain hope.

Gift C: **Giving.** The ability to give your money other resources to be used for God's work.

Gift D: **Teaching.** The ability to teach the Bible in such a way that people learn and grow.

Gift E: **Pastoring.** The ability to effectively guide and care for people in their walk with God.

Gift F: **Mercy.** The ability to act out of compassion toward those who are suffering.

Gift G: **Hospitality.** The gift of being friendly and generous to guests.

Gift H: **Leading.** The ability to motivate others to use their spiritual gifts and to do their best for the work of the Lord.

Gift I: **Evangelism.** The ability to help others come to know Jesus personally.

Gift J: **Faith.** The ability to have a confident belief that God will always do what is the very best.

Assessment

If the score in the Total section is—

12-15: There is strong likelihood that God has blessed you with this spiritual gift.

8-11: There is a reasonable possibility that God has blessed you with this spiritual gift.

4-7: God might be developing this gift in you.

0-4: Your spiritual gifts are probably in a different area than this.

Smile, You've Got Personality

The point
Exploring personality, and how God uses it.

The point, unwrapped
A team of leaders should understand each other's personality (which is fundamentally God's gift to an individual) and appreciate how God uses the team members' similarities and differences.

Where in the word
1 Samuel, Mark, Luke, John, Acts, Galatians

Team Building *10 min.*

Dressing Up
If possible, wear a tux, formal dress, suit, or other clothes appropriate to the dressing up opener. Begin with something like this—

> **How many of you have ever had the privilege of dressing up for a prom, wedding, or formal dinner? In this session we are going to begin our time by dressing each other up with positive comments.**

You'll need—
- strips of paper
- markers
- masking tape

Have your student leaders stand in a circle, then pass out strips of paper, markers, and rolls of masking tape. Ask them to write three positive statements about each student on the team, using a separate strip of paper for each student. The statements should be about inner qualities, such as—

> I really like your sense of humor.

> You're a faithful friend.

> I feel closer to God when I'm around you.

They may want to write the person's name on the back so they know who the comments go to. Emphasize that there should be no put-downs or teasing. Allow them time to think and write.

After your students have finished writing, give them a couple minutes to stick the slips of paper onto the other leaders with pieces of masking tape. Caution them to stick the strips only on appropriate places.

Finally, have your students take their positive messages off and read what the others had to say about them.

Session

Ask your group questions similar to these—

- **What was it like to think of nice things to write about others?**

- **How does it feel to be all dressed up in positive messages?**

- **Did you learn anything new about yourself from what people wrote? If so, what?**

- **Why is it important to tell others the positive things we think of them?**

You'll need—
- copies of **How Has God Wired Me?** (page 85)
- pencils

Team Huddle *15 min.*

How Has God Wired Me?

Explain to your team that in order to make the most of our impact for Jesus Christ, it helps to understand our unique personality traits.

Have your team sit in a circle. Pass out copies of **How Has God Wired Me?** (page 85) and give students a few minutes to read the four styles and choose the one most like them. You may wish to read through the handout with them.

Ask students to sign their names on top of their worksheets and pass them to the person to their right. As leaders receive each worksheet, they should consider the person whose name is at the top and place an X by the personality type they feel best represents that person.

Continue passing handouts to the right until students receive their original worksheets. Have individuals share with the group both how they perceive themselves and how others perceive them.

Ask your group some of these questions—

- **What did you learn about yourself as you considered your personality style?**

- **What do you think of how others on the team perceived you?**

- **What did you learn about others on the team?**

- **What impact could it have on our youth ministry for us to better understand our own and each other's personality styles?**

Explain to your group—

Every great relationship takes a lot of time and effort. Becoming a team doesn't just happen naturally—it's going to take a lot of patience and understanding to be a team that makes an important impact for Christ's kingdom.

- **Your personality style describes your most natural way of relating to others.**

- **Your personality style is unique to you, and it energizes you.**

- **Understanding your own personality style helps you become aware of your strengths and your weaknesses.**

- **Understanding each other's personality styles helps us to have realistic expectations of others.**

82

Team Study *25 min.*

Break up into teams (four is ideal) and hand out **Biblical Personality Profiles** (page 85). Assign each team a person on the handout (Paul, Peter, Nathanael, John the Baptist). Have them read the passages, then using **How Has God Wired Me?** as a reference, determine the personality style of the Bible character they've read about. Tell teams they'll need to report back to the group and explain why they assigned their Bible character that particular style.

After the leaders have shared their findings, summarize with comments like—

- Judging from his letters, **Paul** seemed to have had a powerful, driving personality that enabled him to get the job done and win at all costs. He was very determined to carry out his projects. Paul had a vision and goals—to take the gospel to the Gentiles. God used Paul's power personality to reach the known world.

- **Peter** had a party personality—as soon as he saw Moses and Elijah on the mountain with Jesus, what was his reaction? "Lord this is terrific. Let's stay up here, pitch a tent, and camp out." We also see his ability to stand up in front of others; on the day of Pentecost, 3,000 people joined the Jerusalem church after hearing his sermon. Peter's personality was used by God.

- **Nathanael** had a peaceful personality. It shows up when Jesus complimented him by saying, "Here is a true Israelite, in whom there is nothing false." Jesus praised him for being consistent and balanced. Nathanael was supportive of Jesus. He never asserted himself like Peter did, yet he was there for Jesus. He is there after the resurrection—low-key and supportive. Filled with the Holy Spirit, he offered well-balanced leadership to the early church.

- **John the Baptist** may have had a black-and-white, practical personality. He lived in the wilderness, so he was he was probably withdrawn in his lifestyle. When he called people to repentance, he did it with accuracy and precision. When he was in prison he wanted to know from Jesus himself if he was doing all the right things. When Jesus said he was, he took comfort.

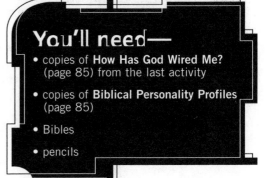

You'll need—
- copies of **How Has God Wired Me?** (page 85) from the last activity
- copies of **Biblical Personality Profiles** (page 85)
- Bibles
- pencils

Encourage students to think about the Bible person who has their same personality style. Ask questions like these—

- What does it mean to you to find a person in the Bible who has your personality style?

- What can you learn from that Bible person about how you can specially minister to others because of your personality style?

God has given each one of us on this leadership team a unique personality. He needs us to be ourselves so he can use us for his purposes.

Session

9

All Together Now

Now that your student leaders have learned more about motivation, spiritual gifts, and personality styles, hand out **Ministry Ideas** (page 86) to each student leader. Prime the pump by having them read through the ideas, then begin brainstorming several ways they can serve the Lord with their motivations, spiritual gifts, and personality styles. Stress that they shouldn't feel locked in to one ministry area. Encourage them to attempt as many ministry positions as necessary to get a feel for where they might minister effectively.

After everyone has listed three ways they can serve the Lord, instruct your student leaders to fill out their **Student Leader Profile** like this:

You'll need—

• copies of **Ministry Ideas** (page 86)

• pencils

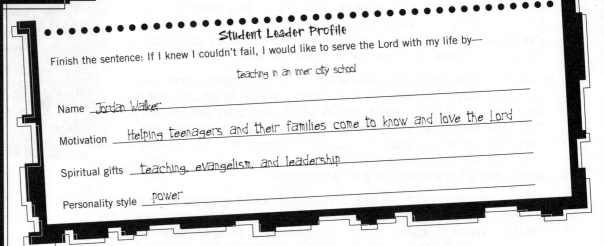

Student Leader Profile

Finish the sentence: If I knew I couldn't fail, I would like to serve the Lord with my life by—

teaching in an inner city school

Name *Jordan Walker*

Motivation *Helping teenagers and their families come to know and love the Lord*

Spiritual gifts *teaching, evangelism, and leadership*

Personality style *power*

Team Prayer 5 min.

Close this session by asking your student leaders to be silent and reflect on this phrase:

One thing I need God to show me is—

After a few minutes of silence have a guided prayer time by praying that phrase. It would help if you, as the leader, would lead the way. You might say—

Lord, one thing I need you to show me is where you are at work in our community. May we join you in your work to reach this city? I trust you God, and I love you.

How Has God Wired Me?

Read through the four personality styles then choose the one most like you.

Party Personality
- Natural strength is friendliness
- Enjoys interacting with people
- Doesn't like to be alone
- Wants to be liked
- Is more people-oriented than task-oriented
- Wants freedom to be creative and spontaneous
- Likes to keep people happy
- Prefers to be up front rather than in the crowd
- Works best in groups

Power Personality
- Natural strength is getting the job completed
- Prefers to lead rather than follow
- Wants to influence others
- Likes having responsibility
- Is persuasive
- Likes seeing the overall picture
- Able to make decisions with or without a group
- Enjoys teaching and being up front

Peaceful Personality
- Natural strength is to be a team player
- Likes to observe and then offer suggestions
- Does not want to stand up in front of a group and lead
- Works well following a leader
- Often can sense how others are doing or feeling
- Prefers a steady and consistent pace
- Able to work alone or in a group
- Is dependable, warm, and easygoing

Practical Personality
- Natural strength is to be task-oriented
- Works well alone
- Sticks with a job until it's done
- Prefers to know and understand the details before moving ahead
- Sees problems as challenges
- Likes to be given responsibility
- Does not like to be put down, even if it's in fun
- Hates being in front of a group

Biblical Personality Profiles

Paul
Read Acts 9:1-2, 28-29 and Galatians 2:11-21
Personality type?

Why?

Nathanael
Read John 1:44-52; 21:1-2, 12-14
Personality type?

Why?

Peter
Read Matthew 17:1-8 and Acts 2:14, 22-41
Personality type?

Why?

John the Baptist
Read Mark 1:2-8 and Luke 7:18-23
Personality type?

Why?

From *Student Leadership Training Manual* by Dennis "Tiger" McLuen & Chuck Wysong. Permission to reproduce this page granted only for use in the buyer's own youth group. www.YouthSpecialties.com

85

Ministry Ideas

Read over this list of potential ministry roles. Add your own ideas to the list. Select at least three roles that match your gifts and personality type.

Paint
Organize prayer groups
Take ets to the homeless
Set up youth group meetings
Bring friends to church
Teach Sunday school
during meetings
Lead a ministry team
Work on a mission trip
Give to the offering
Plan and organize an event
Create mailers and calendars
Follow-up with new people
Greet new people
Make cookies
Listen to others' problems
Share your faith
Help promote youth events
Sponsor a needy child
Maintain equipment or supplies
Write notes to new people
Take pictures
Create bulletin boards
Make posters
Adopt a grandparent
Wash cars for the elderly
Design a youth group logo
Participate in a drama
Play a musical instrument
Lead worship music
Make announcements and introductions

Perform songs by yourself or with others
Baby-sit for free for your youth pastor
Perform office work—word processing, filing, mailing
Videotape events
Organize a slide show or photos
Collect food for the poor
Lead a small group
Share your faith on campus
Clean up after youth programs
Lead a junior high discipleship group
Other ideas:

_____
_____
_____
_____
_____
_____
_____
_____
_____
_____
_____
_____
_____
_____
_____
_____
_____
_____
_____

• •

Student Leader Profile

Finish the sentence: If I knew I couldn't fail, I would like to serve the Lord with my life by—

Name _____

Motivation _____

Spiritual gifts _____

Personality style _____

A Leader's Devotional Life— The Word

The point
Leaders can receive spiritual direction and insight for ministry in the Bible.

The point, unwrapped
Student leaders should commit themselves to spending regular time reading, studying, memorizing, and meditating on the Bible.

Where in the word
Joshua, Mark, 1 Corinthians, 2 Timothy, 2 Peter

Team Building 10 min.

Hidden Books
Distribute pencils and copies of the **Hidden Books** handout (page 90). Instruct your students to read the paragraph silently and look for 18 books from the Bible, circling the ones they find.

After a few minutes ask your team—

- **How many books did you find?**

- **Which ones did you find?** *See the sample for these answers: Mark, Luke, Acts, Revelation, James, Ruth, Numbers, Job, Amos, Esther, Judges, Titus, Lamentations, Hebrews, Joel, Haggai, Nahum, Chronicle(s)*

- **Describe what you did to find these books.**

This exercise is a lot like reading the Bible. We can see pages of words as we read, but we often miss the message behind them. Psalm 119:105 says, "Your word is a lamp to my feet and a light for my path." In this session we will learn about how to how to read, study, and apply God's Word to our lives.

You'll need—
- copies of **Hidden Books** (page 90)
- pencils

I once made some remarks about hidden books in the Bible. It was a lulu! Kept some people looking so hard for facts and studying for the revelation. They were in a jam, especially since the books were not capitalized, but the truth finally struck numbers of readers. To others, it was a real job. We want it to be a most fascinating few moments for you. Yes, there will be some really easy to spot; others require judges to determine. We must admit it usually takes a minute to find one and then there will be loud lamentations when you see how simple it is. One lady says she brews coffee while she puzzles her brain. Another "Joe" looks for a gimmick. Ah, but it can be done by an old hag. Gain may come slowly, but it's as easy as peeling a banana. Hum a tune while you rack your brain with this chronicle. Happy hunting!

Team Huddle *5 min.*

Opinions!

Use this informative mixer to give your students an opportunity to find out about each other's opinions. Break up into groups of four, and have each student give a one-word opinion about—

- School   • Government   • MTV   • The Bible

When students have finished sharing, continue with questions and comments along this line—

- **To what degree did your group members agree or disagree on the four issues you discussed?**

- **Why do you think people tend to heat up about their opinions and feel so strongly about certain issues?**

- **Just where did you get—or how did you form—your opinions on the matters you discussed?**

Now let's go to a subject that our society really has strong and divergent opinions about: religion. We're famous for disagreeing about the large and small matters of faith. It seems, for example, that even those who agree about Christianity's big issues (our need for God, the deity of Jesus, the truth of the Bible) still disagree about the details (does God also need us? Exactly when did Jesus "become" God? How can the Bible be true about matters that didn't even exist when it was written?).

Take the Bible—everyone agrees it's an ancient book. Some people dismiss it as just an ancient book, irrelevant for today. Some classify it as story and myth. Others virtually worship the Bible. Which of these opinions is true?

To find out, let's discover what the Bible says about itself.

You'll need—

- whiteboard and markers
- bar of soap still sealed in the original wrapper
- copies of **Bible Alive! [overview]** (page 91)
- copies of **Bible Alive! [worksheet]** (page 92), three per student
- Bibles
- pencils

Team Study *30 min.*

Ask for volunteers to read 2 Timothy 3:16-17, Joshua 1:8, 2 Peter 1:20-21, and 1 Corinthians 2:12-14. Have students answer questions like these, as you jot key words or phrases on the board—

- **What observations do you have about us and the Bible from these verses?**

- **Are there any contradictions in these passages? Like what?**

- **Which verses seems most important to you? Why?**

- **Has your perception about the Bible changed after reading these verses?**

- **After reading these verses, what do you think you should do? What do you think God wants you to do?**

Zestfully Clean

After discussing the questions, hold up a bar of soap still in its box.

> How is God's Word like this bar of soap? This soap has the power to clean you and remove dirt from your body. Inside this wrapper is a bar that contains the chemicals needed to clean your body. But as long as the bar is in this wrapper, the chemicals are useless. For me to release the power of the soap to clean, I need to take the bar out of the wrapper and apply the soap to my body.
>
> God's Word is exactly like that. God's Word has the power to transform your life. It's sharper than any two-edged sword, but as long as it sits unopened—the power can never be released. God's Word is living and active; but in order to release the power, you need to open it up, read it, and, most importantly, apply it to your life.

Inductive Bible Study Worksheet

Continue by saying—

> But where do we start? The Bible has 66 books. It was written in a different time and culture. Sometimes this book can seem intimidating. Today I'll introduce you to a three-step process that can help the Bible come alive for you and make a difference in your life.

Have the students remain in their teams and distribute **Bible Alive! [overview]** (page 91). Ask them to turn in their Bibles to John 3:16-17, and apply the steps outlined on the handout. After a few minutes, have each team report its findings.

Now express the following idea to your team—

> The Bible is God's love letter to us. This three-point outline of observe, interpret, and apply can be used to help us better understand and apply God's Word for our lives. Mark Twain once said, "Most people are bothered by those passages of Scripture they do not understand, but the passages that bother me are those I do understand."
>
> As modern Christian leaders we see that few things are more important in this day and age than for us in leadership to know God and his plan for our lives and this world. One of the ways that we get to know him is through his Word. In the next session we'll learn the importance of having a conversation with God through prayer, but for now let's take the Bible challenge.

Give each student leader 3 copies of the **Bible Alive! [worksheet]** (page 92). Ask them to use the six passages listed on **Bible Alive! [overview]** for study this week, one each day. You may want to make next week's lesson a time of feedback and sharing about what they learned. Challenge your students to spend 10 to 15 minutes a day reading the Bible and whatever time it takes to apply it to their lives.

Team Prayer *5 min.*

Have your student leaders form pairs who will commit to become accountability and prayer partners that help each other work on their Bible passages this week. Close in prayer as a team, asking God to help student leaders read, understand, and apply his Word for their lives.

Hidden Books

Find and circle the names of 18 books in the Bible.

I once made some remarks about hidden books in the Bible. It was a lulu! Kept some people looking so hard for facts and studying for the revelation. They were in a jam, especially since the books were not capitalized, but the truth finally struck numbers of readers. To others, it was a real job. We want it to be a most fascinating few moments for you. Yes, there will be some really easy to spot; others require judges to determine. We must admit it usually takes a minute to find one and then there will be loud lamentations when you see how simple it is. One lady says she brews coffee while she puzzles her brain. Another "Joe" looks for a gimmick. Ah, but it can be done by an old hag. Gain may come slowly, but it's as easy as peeling a banana. Hum a tune while you rack your brain with this chronicle. Happy hunting!

Bible Alive!
[overview]

Before you begin, pray for God's Spirit to guide you as you read his love letter to you.

Day 1 Mark 1:1-13	Day 2 Mark 1:14-34	Day 3 Mark 1:35-45
Day 4 Mark 2:1-12	Day 5 Mark 2:13-22	Day 6 Mark 2:23-28

Observation—What's going on in the passage?
Step 1. Read with an open mind.
Step 2. Record the facts (Who? What? When? Where? Why? So what?).

-
-
-

-
-
-

Interpretation—What does it mean?
Step 1. What does it say about God?

Step 2. What does it say about me?

Step 3. Look up unfamiliar words in dictionary or Bible dictionary.

Application—What should I do?
Step 1. Ask and answer these questions:

Is there a challenge to accept?

Is there an attitude to change?

Is there a command to obey?

Is there a sin to avoid?

Is there a promise to claim?

Is there an example to follow?

How can I apply this to my life?

Step 2. Describe it.

How can I make this passage personal?

How can I make it practical?

Step 3. Memorize it.
Each week choose a verse or passage that impacts you personally and memorize it. One or two verses a week is a steady pace—but if you're motivated to do more, go for it! The important thing is to spend time each day reviewing the verses you've already memorized as you add new ones to memory.

Step 4. Meditate on it.
Review God's Word to you throughout the day.

Bible Alive!
[worksheet]

Date

Bible reference

Observation. What does it say?

Interpretation. What does it mean?

Application. What should I do?

Key Verse. What is the key verse of the passage?

Bible Alive!
[worksheet]

Date

Bible reference

Observation. What does it say?

Interpretation. What does it mean?

Application. What should I do?

Key Verse? What is the key verse of the passage?

A Leader's Devotional Life— Prayer

The point
Want to minister as a student leader? Start with listening to and conversing with God.

The point, unwrapped
Your student leaders need to cultivate a daily, personal time of prayer.

Where in the word
Psalms, Isaiah, Jeremiah, Matthew, Luke, John, Philippians, 1 Thessalonians, 1 Timothy, 1 John, Revelation

Team Building *10 min.*

Who Am I?
Pass out index cards and pencils and have your students record three little-known facts about themselves. For example, "I once went up in a hot air balloon," or "I almost drowned when I was 11 years old." Have everyone sign their cards and pass them in.

Shuffle the cards, then read them aloud one at a time. See if the group can guess the identity of the author. Interesting facts will come to light, and students will be amazed to discover new insights about their friends.

For a twist, put a card in the stack with three little-known facts about Jesus Christ. For example—

- I fell asleep on a boat trip one time during a violent storm.
- When I was twelve my parents left on a trip and forgot me.
- I prayed for a man and God miraculously healed him.

When you've gone through all the cards, ask—

- **Did any of the things you learned change what you think or feel about someone in the room? Explain your answer.**

- **How does this activity shed light about our need to know God better?**

You know, sometimes we think we know people, and then we learn amazing new facts about them that make us appreciate them all the more. In the same way, we may think we know God, but there are always new insights to gain and ways to deepen our relationship with him. And knowing God better is essential to living and ministering in ways that please him. In this session we'll look at the importance of an ongoing prayer life with God.

You'll need—
- index cards, one per student
- pencils

Team Huddle *30 min.*

Too Much Prayer?

Read the following story or tell it in your own words:

Johnny, a very bright five-year-old, told his daddy he'd like to have a baby brother and, along with his request, offered to do whatever he could to help. His dad, a very bright 35-year-old, paused for a moment and then replied, "I'll tell you what, Johnny. If you pray every day for two months for a baby brother, I guarantee that God will give you one!" Johnny responded eagerly to his dad's challenge and went to his bedroom early that night to start praying for a baby brother.

He prayed every night for a whole month, but after that time, he began to get skeptical. He checked around the neighborhood and found out that what he thought was going to happen had never occurred in the history of the neighborhood. You don't just pray for two months and then, whammo—a new baby brother. So Johnny quit praying.

After another month, Johnny's mother went to the hospital. When she came back home, Johnny's parents called him into the bedroom. He walked into the room, not expecting to find anything, but there was a little bundle lying right next to his mother. His dad pulled back the et and there was—not one baby brother, but two! His mother had twins!

Johnny's dad looked at him and said, "Now aren't you glad you prayed?" Johnny hesitated a little and then looked up at his dad and said, "Yes I am, but aren't you glad I quit praying when I did?"

As a group describe prayer to a five-year-old like Johnny. List ideas on a whiteboard. Then conclude with comments like—

Johnny's dad knew in advance that Johnny's prayer would be answered according to his wish. And our heavenly Father knows in advance whether or not he'll answer our prayers according to our desires too. He can see the future and he knows our true wants and needs—even before we ask. So why should we bother to pray?

You'll need—
• whiteboard and markers

From *More Hot Illustrations for Youth Talks* by Wayne Rice, Youth Specialties, 1995.

Team Study *15 min.*

Divide the group into four teams, perhaps by the first letter of students' last names (A-F, G-M, N-S, and T-Z). Distribute copies of **A Leader's Devotional Life—Prayer** (page 96). Instruct teams to take about eight minutes or so to look up the Bible references you've assigned to them, answer the questions posed, and then prepare a one-minute summary to present to the entire group.

You'll need—
• copies of **A Leader's Devotional Life—Prayer** (page 96)

• whiteboard and markers

• Bibles

• pencils

Talkback

Allow individual groups to share their findings in a one-minute summaries with the entire leadership team.

After students have finished their presentations, have them collaborate to create a one-sentence summary of everything they learned about prayer. Write the sentence on the whiteboard. Then ask—

- **Based on this sentence about prayer, what role does prayer need to play in our individual lives?**

- **What has this activity taught you about prayer?**

- **Will you make any changes in your prayer life as a result of what you've learned today? Why or why not?**

- **What role does prayer need to play in our youth ministry and our student leadership team?**

- **Do we need to make any changes in the way we pray? If so, what changes should we make?**

Conclude this section by saying something like—

It's been said that, **"When we work, we work; but when we pray, God works."** Prayer releases the power of God. We can release that power as we approach God with all our needs and plans for our youth ministry.

But prayer is more than making requests; it's an intimate and loving relationship with the Creator of the universe. To be a leader for God we need to be in conversation with him on a regular basis.

One person asked the question, "When should we pray?" The answer is, "Before we do anything else." As important as it is that you pray at our weekly student leadership meetings, how you pray between our meetings is much more important. This year we want to raise the standard in our prayer lives.

Take the Prayer Challenge

Distribute **Take the Prayer Challenge** (page 97) to your student leaders. Challenge your team with a statement like this—

You'll need—
- copies of **Take the Prayer Challenge** (page 97)

This week before you go to school or before you go to bed at night, practice praying for five to 10 minutes with this weekly prayer guide. Each day of the week will have a different prayer focus and concern. Have fun and pray hard.

Team Prayer *10 min.*

End your session with prayer.

You may want to guide students through the prayer by specifically directing them through the proces of praise, repentance, asking for others, and asking for themselves. See the **Mini Prayer Retreat** (pages 225-230) for more details.

A Leader's Devotional Life—Prayer

Read the verses and finish the accompanying sentence in each section.

WHAT IS PRAYER?

Read Matthew 7:7-11, John 15:5-7, Revelation 3:20, and 1 John 4:19.
(*abide* or *dwell* means not just to know about God, but to know him in a personal way.)
In your own words finish this sentence:

Prayer is—

WHY SHOULD WE PRAY?

Read John 16:23-24, Psalm 42:1-2, Psalm 103:1-5, and Jeremiah 29:11-12.
In your own words finish this sentence:

We should pray because—

WHEN CAN WE PRAY?

Read 1 Thessalonians 5:17, Luke 18:1-8, Psalm 5:3, Psalm 88:1, Philippians 4:6, and 1 Timothy 2:1.
In your own words finish this sentence:

We can pray—

HOW CAN WE PRAY?

Read Psalm 9:1-2, 1 John 1:9, 1 Thessalonians 5:18, Isaiah 41:1, and Matthew 7:7-11.
In your own words finish this sentence:

Prayer is—

Take the Prayer Challenge

Monday	Pray for ministers and missionaries.
Tuesday	Pray for trials that you—or a friend—are facing today.
Wednesday	Pray for world concerns.
Thursday	Pray prayers of thanksgiving.
Friday	Pray for your family.
Saturday	Pray for our church members and other Christians around the world.
Sunday	Pray for the salvation of family members and friends.

✂ -

Take the Prayer Challenge

Monday	Pray for ministers and missionaries.
Tuesday	Pray for trials that you—or a friend—are facing today.
Wednesday	Pray for world concerns.
Thursday	Pray prayers of thanksgiving.
Friday	Pray for your family.
Saturday	Pray for our church members and other Christians around the world.
Sunday	Pray for the salvation of family members and friends.

Session 12

A Leader's Devotional Life— Time with God

The point
If you want to know how to minister as a student leader, spend time with God.

The point, unwrapped
Students should nurture a devotional life if they want to recognize direction and insight for their lives and ministries.

Where in the word
Psalms, Matthew, Mark, Colossians

Team Building *10 min.*

Getting My Priorities Straight
Divide students into groups of four or so. Be sure each group has a Bible and each student has a pencil and a copy of **Let's Talk, God** (page 102). Let one student read the monolog (you can have a second student read the italicized words, if you want) and discuss the questions in their small groups.

Team Huddle *30 min.*
Have a leader summarize what *time with God* means. Some people use the terms *devotions* or *quiet time* as a time set aside each day to listen to and communicate with God through prayer and Bible study. Continue by asking your students some more questions, perhaps these:

- **Why is prioritizing time with God on a regular basis important?**

- **What would help you touch base with God more regularly?**

- **Why is time with God even more important for a leader than for other Christians?**

Ask your leaders to open their Bibles to Mark 1:35. Say something like—

In this passage Jesus models for us the importance for a leader to be in prayer. It says, "Very early in the morning, while it was still dark, Jesus got up, left the house and went off to a solitary place, where he prayed." Jesus made time to be with his Father. He would miss sleep to do it if necessary. Just think—if the Son of God needed to make time for private devotions, how much more do we need to do it?

You'll need—
- copies of **Let's Talk, God** (page 102)

You'll need—
- copies of **31 Flavors of Daily Time with God** (page 103)
- copies of **Praying with Power** (page 104)
- Bibles
- pencils
- whiteboard and markers

Ask your team questions like these—

- **Sometimes spending time with God regularly is a challenge. Why do you think that's so?**

- **Go out on a limb. Do you regularly spend time with God? Why or why not?**

- **What helps you? What makes it hard for you?**

- **What should you do during your time with God? Why do you think so?**

After your team gives you several answers, introduce or summarize the following points for them.

- *Find a time and place.* **Think of your day. When is the best time for an uninterrupted and consistent regular meeting with God? There isn't a correct time. Some people prefer the morning, others find that evenings work better. The point is to have your time with God whenever you can concentrate best. Don't squeeze it in. Make it a priority and build your day around it.**

   Once you find that time, find a quiet, private place and designate it as your meeting place with God. Some suggestions for a place could be your car, your bedroom, a special place in your house, or a quiet corner of a library. Whenever possible, have your time alone with God in the same place each day. If you miss your set-aside time, still spend time with God later on the same day.

- *Fight for that time.* **Carl Jung said, "Hurry, worry, and noise are not things of the devil—they *are* the devil." If the devil can keep us in such a hurry that we don't have time for God or if we are so worried that we won't trust God or if we're surrounded by so much noise that we can't hear God, then the devil is doing his job. Once we set our time to meet with God we need to fight for that time.**

- *Feed on God's Word.* **Just as our physical bodies need food to keep us going throughout the day, our spiritual bodies need regular spiritual food to keep us going and growing throughout our day as well. We need to be taking in regular doses of God's Word. Read Psalm 119: 9-11.**

- *Follow a plan.* **In this session and the last, we reviewed the power of prayer and God's Word, two essential elements to incorporate into your time with God.**

Now tell your students you'd like to brainstorm different ways to have a devotional time, one for each day of the month. Encourage leaders to use their imaginations and be creative. Have them read the ideas already listed on **31 Flavors of Daily Time with God** (page 103) to get their creativity flowing. Then ask them to record their ideas at the bottom.

After a few minutes, have students share their best suggestions. Now you might say—

Having a daily time in prayer and in God's Word is vital for every growing Christian. In closing, let's put it all together.

Distribute **Praying with Power** (page 104), and go over it with the students. They can make notes on the handout as you go along. The text of the handout is listed below with a few additional comments you can use to elaborate on each category. Write the key words on a whiteboard as you mention them.

- **Praise.** Begin your time with God by praising God for who he is: "You are a holy God; You are a God of love; You are all-powerful." God is worthy of our praise.
- **Silence.** Be silent and still, knowing you've come before your Lord. Ask him to guide you in your time with him today.
- **Confession.** Ask God to reveal any thoughts, spoken words, or actions that need to be confessed. Read Psalm 139:23-24.
- **Read God's Word.** Read one of the Gospels or Psalms using the **Bible Alive! [worksheet]** from session 10.
- **Pray God's Word.** Augustine said the Bible was written *to* us but the Psalms were written *for* us. Personalize a psalm or a passage from the Bible and pray God's Word back to him.
- **Meditate.** Focus in on a key verse or two. Reflect on it, perhaps emphasizing a different word each time through so you can consider the variations in meaning. You can meditate on verses throughout out the day.
- **Pray for others.** Specifically pray for the needs of family and friends.
- **Pray for yourself.** Specifically pray for your needs, your day, and for God's guidance in your life.
- **Thanksgiving.** Thank God for what he's done in your life.
- **Sing.** The Bible says to "make a joyful noise" to the Lord. Sing songs you've heard in youth group meetings or church.
- **Silence.** Reflecting back on your time with the Lord, ask Jesus to guide you and reveal himself throughout your day—"God, wherever you are moving today, that is where I want to be."
- **Commit.** As you go, surrender your day to the Lord and commit to him again your heart and life. You can say something like this, "Lord, help me to not be ashamed of the Gospel. I want to be ready to share the good news I have at any time. Amen."

Time with God Contract

Some students appreciate the accountability of a contract. Pass out copies of the **Time with God Contract** (page 105) and read through it. Emphasize its short-term duration—one week only—and that it is strictly voluntarily. Stress that students should agree to participate in the contract willingly with a full commitment to fulfilling their part of the agreement.

Have the participants (only) determine consequences to fulfilling and not fulfilling their part. Have students sign their copies of the contract and turn them in (or you may want them to keep the contract to remind themselves, and you keep a list of participants' names).

You'll need—
- copies of **Time with God Contract** (page 105)
- pencils

Team Prayer *10 min.*

Move into a time of silence, asking God to give the students strength to live up to the commitments they've just made. Close by asking God to bless the student leaders through their commitments this week.

Let's Talk, God

But seek first his kingdom and his righteousness, and all these things will be given to you as well.

—Matthew 6:33

I don't know about you, but I can't figure out why God doesn't talk to people today like he did in the Bible. I mean, my youth pastor tells us these stories of Moses or whoever chatting with God, as if the two of them were sitting across the table from each other: "So what do you think about this, God?" No, don't do that. "Oh, okay…then what about that?" Yup, that's exactly the thing to do. "Great. Thanks, God. Catch you later." Meanwhile, I feel like I spend half my life groping like a blind person from decision to decision. My youth pastor tells us to "walk with God"…I'd love to, but God doesn't seem to want to walk with me. At least in a way I can recognize. In fact, I could swear he's playing hide-and-seek with me, teasing me along, giving me far fewer answers than I need, showing himself to me only enough to keep me from bagging the whole thing.

Then a great and powerful wind tore the mountains apart and shattered the rocks before the Lord, but the Lord was not in the wind. After the wind there was an earthquake, but the Lord was not in the earthquake. After the earthquake came a fire, but the Lord was not in the fire. And after the fire came a gentle whisper. When Elijah heard it, he pulled his cloak over his face and went out and stood at the mouth of the cave.
Then a voice said to him, "What are you doing here, Elijah?" (1 Kings 19:11-13)

Be still, and know that I am God. (Psalm 46:10)

In repentance and rest is your salvation, in quietness and trust is your strength. (Isaiah 30:15)

Second only to suffering, waiting may be the greatest teacher and trainer in godliness, maturity, and genuine spirituality most of us ever encounter. (Richard Hendrix)

- What does *time with God* mean?
- What ideas do you get about spending time with God from reading the Bible verses and other texts on this page? Can you list some general principles that apply?
- Can you think of other verses that might add to the discussion? What issues do the verses raise?
- Which verse seems most important to you?

31 Flavors of Daily Time with God

1. Read five Psalms a day for a month. (You can read the whole book in 30 days.)

2. Start a prayer journal. Write down prayer requests and answered prayers.

3. Use the *One-Minute Bible* (Broadman & Holman, 1998) to get a good overview of the Bible in a year.

4. Use A *Time with God Bible* (Word, 1991) to read through the New Testament.

5. Write poetry of praise or a letter to God.

6. Write down verses on index cards. You can refer to them during the day.

7. Meet two other friends and form a prayer triplet and pray together each week.

8. Read a chapter of Proverbs each day (for example, read Proverbs 15 on the 15th, Proverbs 27 on the 27th).

9. Take a walk with God and talk to him as you would a friend.

10. Get out in the country or by the ocean. Meditate on words from the Bible and reflect on God's creation.

11. Write a song about your love for God.

12. Draw a picture of God's creation, the cross, or the empty tomb.

13. Read a chapter a day from Oswald Chambers' classic, *My Utmost for His Highest* (Discovery House, 1963).

14. Use a devotional guide, such as *The Call to Prayer: Youth Journal*, by Lloyd Ogilvie and Chuck Wysong (Harvest House, 1998) or *Youthwalk* magazine (Walk Through the Bible, www.youthwalk.org).

15.

16.

17.

18.

19.

20.

21.

22.

23.

24.

25.

26.

27.

28.

29.

30.

31.

Praying with Power

_____
date

- **Praise**
- **Silence**
- **Confession**
- **Read God's Word** Bible passage: _____

    Observation—_What does it say?_

    Interpretation—_What does it mean?_

    Application—_What should I do?_

- **Pray God's Word** Bible passage: _____

- **Meditate** Bible verse: _____

- **Pray for others** Prayer requests:
    -
    -
    -

- **Pray for myself** Prayer requests:
    -
    -
    -

- **Thanksgiving** What you're thankful for:
    -
    -
    -

- **Song**
- **Silence**
- **Commitment**

Time with God Contract

I, _____ , do hereby contract with the other

members of the _____
name of youth group

student leadership team to have a daily quiet time for each of the next seven days, beginning

_____ and ending

_____

    In signing this agreement, I am requesting the group's active support, encouragement,

and accountability. Should I fail to live up to this contract, I agree to face the consequences agreed

upon by the group, namely,

_____

_____

_____

_____

      Signed on this _____ day of _____ in the year _____

_____
name

_____
leader's signature

Facing Temptation

The point
Be prepared for excruciating temptation.

The point, unwrapped
If Jesus Christ himself was tempted, then Christian leaders should not think themselves exempt from temptations of every kind. Your students can be at least somewhat prepared for what they will face, and understand the biblical nuts and bolts of resisting temptation.

Where in the word
Judges, Psalms, Matthew, 1 Corinthians, Galatians, Hebrews, James

Team Building *15 min.*

To Diet or Not to Diet? That Is the Question!
Read the following story or tell it in your own words—

> There once was a man who always stopped by a bakery on his way to work in the morning to pick up some goodies for the staff coffee break. He finally decided to go on a diet. In order to avoid the temptation to eat rich sweets, he began taking a different route to work so he didn't have to go by the bakery and be tempted. The entire office staff encouraged him as he dieted.
>
> One day, however, he had to do an errand on his way to work and it was in the neighborhood of the bakery. As he approached the bakery he said to himself, "Maybe God wants me to stop by the bakery this morning and pick up some goodies for the office staff." So he prayed, "Lord, if you want me to stop at the bakery this morning, make a parking spot available right in front of the bakery so there is no question in my mind." And sure enough, there it was—a parking spot, right in front of the bakery, on his sixth trip around the block.

Here are some questions to get your discussion started—

- **What do you think of the man's reasoning as he approached the bakery?**
- **Do you think he really wanted to avoid the temptation? Why or why not?**
- **If he had really wanted to avoid the temptation, what could he have done differently?**
- **What situations are most tempting for you? Why are they so tempting?**
- **When you face temptation, how do you handle it?**

Explain that today we're going to be discussing temptation and looking at ways we can resist temptation, even when there doesn't seem to be a way out.

Team Huddle *15 min.*

Distribute **The Temptation Quiz** (page 111) and pencils to your students and have them fill it out individually. When students have finished, invite them to share their responses to the questions. Use their responses as springboards for further discussion and ask some questions along these lines—

- **What are the most common temptations people in the world face?**
- **What are the most common temptations people in your school face?**
- **Is there any one person or group of people that faces more temptation than the rest of the world? Why do you think that?**
- **What makes temptation so difficult to resist?**
- **What are some good ways for dealing with temptation?**

Now look a little more closely, and personally, at temptation. Distribute **Facing Temptation** (page 112) and have the kids get together in groups of three. (To encourage students to share more freely regarding this discussion, groups can be made up of members of the same sex.) Ask them to come up with the top five temptations that their closest friends face, then the top three temptations that they face.

Gather the team together, and discuss in what ways (if any) their individual temptations differed from the temptations of other students at their school or even from their closest friends. If applicable, ask students why they face different temptations than their friends.

Team Study *15 min.*

You can begin by saying something like—

We all face temptations. Although our temptations might not be exactly the same as those of other people around us, they're still temptations. We're going to take a look at Jesus and some of the temptations he faced and try to learn from his example how we can resist them.

Divide the whole group into three teams. Each group should take five minutes to read one portion from the temptation of Jesus and be prepared to report back to the entire group on the answers to the first four questions.

Then have everyone return to their original group and answer the questions about their own top three temptations.

After the groups have had time to discuss the questions, summarize the following points for your students:

Jesus was the Son of God, yet he had to face temptations. As a matter of fact, Hebrews 4:15-16 tells us that Jesus was tempted in every way we are tempted, yet he did not give in and sin. Because of this Jesus understands what we're going through when we're tempted.

Here are four things that can help you overcome the temptations you face.
[You may write these on the whiteboard for emphasis and encourage your students to take notes on their handouts.]

- *Don't play around with temptation.* Stay as far away from tempting situations as you possibly can rather than living in the danger zone. Remember Samson? (Read Judges 13:2-5, 24-25; 14:1-20; 16:4-21.) He just couldn't resist the temptation of a beautiful woman. First his wife and then Delilah deceived him for their own personal gain. Both times he eventually gave in to temptation and told them what they wanted to know, but it took the women several tries to wear Samson down. He should have seized the opportunity to get up and get out while he still could. But Samson either thought he was too strong (physically and mentally) to be overtaken or too smart to be outwitted. As it turned out, he was neither.

Our temptations can be just as deceptive. Don't underestimate the power of what tempts you or overestimate your ability to resist it.

- *Resist temptation with all your might.* James 4:7 tells us to "submit yourselves, then, to God. Resist the devil, and he will flee from you." We will never resist temptation unless we get serious about it. 1 Corinthians 10:13 says, "No temptation has seized you except what is common to man. And God is faithful; he will not let you be tempted beyond what you can bear. But when you are tempted, he will also provide a way out so that you can stand up under it." So when you are tempted, look for the way out that God has provided for you.

- *Remind yourself of the end result.* When we give into temptation it's usually because we look at the immediate and pleasurable side of the sin and forget to think about the long-term consequences. Galatians 6:7-8 says, "Do not be deceived: God cannot be mocked. A man reaps what he sows. The one who sows to please his sinful nature, from that nature will reap destruction; the one who sows to please the Spirit, from the Spirit will reap eternal life."

It's tough for teens to believe that bad things may happen to them, but especially as a result of their own actions. They love to live for the moment! But what seems like little, harmless things can and will ultimately lead to painful consequences down the road—and not only for the one who sins. Eventually these tiny sins get out of control and they end up affecting entire families, groups of friends, youth groups, and schools. Sin has both long-term and far-reaching effects. Past sins can haunt you the rest of your life and cause a painful ripple effect throughout the lives of many people you know and love.

We don't *want* to think about the bad stuff that might happen, so we shut our eyes and dive headfirst into the good stuff. Reminding ourselves of the end result of sin should make it easier for us to resist temptation.

- *Protect your mind.* There are so many things around us that can pollute our minds and make it easier for us to give into temptation, but by making the Bible a greater part of our lives we can gain the strength we need to overcome the temptations we face. Psalm 119:9-11 says, "How can a young man keep his way pure? By living according to your word. I seek you with all my heart; do not let me stray from your commands. I have hidden your word in my heart that I might not sin against you."

Temptation is a very serious issue in a Christian's life. We must be on our guard at all times, know what standard of behavior God expects of us, be aware of the things that can most easily drag us down and cause us to sin, and be ready to flee when temptation rears its ugly head. We also need to be ready to ask God to forgive us when we slip, forgive ourselves, and start over, as many times as necessary.

After you've summarized the information above, ask some questions like—

- **Why is it especially important that leaders resist temptation?**

- **How can our team help one another resist temptation?**

Team Prayer *20 min.*

Begin by separating the team into single-gender prayer groups. Have them pray for the temptations the members of the group are feeling and for the strength to overcome their temptations. Bring the entire group back together and spend time praying about anything that is on their hearts.

The Temptation Quiz

Answer the following questions.

1. When faced with a choice between giving into a temptation or resisting it, I usually— (circle all
responses that apply)
Flip a coin to help me decide
Run and hide under my bed
Think it over
Pray and ask God to show me what to do
Talk it over with a good friend
Other _____

2. I (circle one) often/sometimes/never feel tempted to do something that others are doing in
order to be accepted.

3. There is a right and a wrong choice for each decision I must make. _____ Yes _____ No

4. All temptation is a sin. _____ Yes _____ No

5. The temptation I face most often is—

6. In order of their importance to you, list five values or priorities in your life that you could rely on
to guide you when you're face to face with a temptation.
1.

2.

3.

4.

5.

Facing Temptation

You've brainstormed some ideas about the temptations that people around the world and in your school face. Now let's get personal. Share your answers to these questions with your partners.

• List the top five temptations that you think your closest friends face.

• List the top three temptations that you face in your life.

Read one of the following texts (as your leader assigns them) and answer the questions. Report your findings to the entire group.

Matthew 4:1-4   **Matthew 4:5-7**   **Matthew 4:8-11**

a. What did Satan tempt Jesus to do?

b. What did Satan promise Jesus he would gain?

c. Why would it be wrong for Jesus to do what he was tempted to do?

d. How did Jesus respond?

Return to your small groups to discuss the following questions.

• What is Satan tempting you to do (you might want to refer to the three temptations you listed above)?

• What is Satan promising that you will gain by giving in to these temptations?

• Why would it be wrong for you to give in?

• What would Jesus do? What's the right response for you?

Becoming a Praying Team

The point
Praying together.

The point, unwrapped
The Lord's Prayer is a model for the prayers of Christian leaders. Your students will explore the elements in this prayer and try their hand at conversational prayer as a form of group prayer.

Where in the word
Matthew

Team Building *15 min.*

Questions and Answers
Before the meeting, get a small, square box or a wooden cube that can be held in one hand. If your group has more that 12 students in it, you'll probably want to divide into smaller groups and provide one box for each group.

Write each of the following phrases on square slips of paper, and tape or glue each slip to one side of the cube:

YES, BUT I'LL NEVER DO THAT AGAIN

BECAUSE I WAS CURIOUS

YES, AND I'D DO THAT AGAIN IF I COULD

NO, AND I NEVER WOULD

BECAUSE MY PARENTS TOLD ME TO

YES, BUT I DON'T KNOW WHY

> ### You'll need—
> • a cube with a question written on each side, created ahead of time according to directions

Ask students to get into their groups and give each one an answer cube. Give each leader a turn rolling the cube. After a roll of the cube, the person must come up with a question that goes with the answer that ends up on top. For example, for the phrase, "Because I was curious," they might come up with a question like, "Why did I put my hand in the VCR and get it stuck when I was three?" The questions have to be about real events in the students' lives. Play as many rounds as you have time for.

Then ask questions like these—

• **What was it like to have the answer before you created the question?**

• **How is this like how we approach God with our prayers? How is it different?**

• **What attitude should we have when we pray?**

Discuss with the group how sometimes we go to God to ask for his guidance when we've already come up with our own answer. This happens when we want something so badly that we ask God to do something as a sign—often something that might happen anyway—to reassure ourselves that God wants the same thing for us and therefore it *can't* be wrong.

So Evan might pray something like, "Dear God, you know how much I like Haley. If you want me to ask her to the dance, give me a sign. Make the telephone ring in the next two hours, and then I'll know that you want me to call her." In this case Evan is trying to use a ringing telephone to boost his courage to call a girl. He doesn't really want to know what God thinks about Haley or about him taking her to the dance.

Ask your students for more examples of this type of prayer and whether they've ever used it themselves.

You'll need—

- copies of **Becoming a Praying Team** (page 117)
- pencils
- whiteboard and markers

Team Huddle 15 min.
Instruct your team along these lines—

If you agree with the following statement I'm going to read, give me a thumbs up. If you disagree, give me a thumbs down. *Prayer is one of the most important things we can do in our lives, and it deserves to be given a high priority every day.*

Continue this polling activity by asking leaders to respond to each of the following statements or any others you come up with:

- **If you spend more time praying than doing anything else, put your thumbs up.**
- **If you spend more time praying than eating, put your thumbs up.**
- **If you spend more time praying than you spend with your friends, put your thumbs up.**
- **If you spend more time praying than watching TV, put your thumbs up.**
- **If you spend more time praying than eating asparagus, put your thumbs up.**

Depending on your polling results, you can say something like—

A minute ago we all agreed that prayer was one of the most important things we can do in our lives, yet most of us have just indicated that the only thing that gets a smaller amount of our time is eating asparagus. Why do you think there is such a difference in what we believe about prayer and what we do?

Distribute **Becoming a Praying Team** (page 117) and pencils. Have your student leaders answer the first three questions. Then have leaders share their answers to the first question; as they do, list on a whiteboard the things that keep them from praying, make it difficult for them to pray, or interfere with their efforts to pray.

Help students talk about their experiences with prayer, starting with stories about the prayers God has answered. Ask your students questions like—

- **What did it feel like when God answered your prayers?**
- **How did your answered prayers affect your prayer life?**

Then invite students to share stories about prayers that God has not answered. You could ask similar questions like these—

- **How did you feel when you realized God didn't answer your prayer?**

- **How did this experience affect your prayer life?**

To wrap up this section and transition into the next one, say something like—

> **Prayer is a tough thing to fit into our busy lives and hectic schedules, and it can become more difficult when we feel like God says no to our requests. One way to increase the amount of time we spend praying during the week is to hold each other accountable to regularly pray together as a team. We can easily do this by making prayer a top priority during our weekly student leadership meetings.**
>
> **If we're going to make the effort to pray more often, then maybe we should take a look at how Jesus instructed his own leadership team—the disciples—to pray, and then try to follow their example.**

Team Study 15 min.

You could introduce this section by saying—

> **One day after Jesus had been praying and returned to be with the disciples, they said to him, "Lord, teach us to pray." When Jesus' disciples asked him to teach them to pray, he didn't say, "Oh, you know how to pray" or "Just pray any way you feel like praying." Instead he responded to their request by giving them a model prayer which is referred to as the Lord's Prayer. This model prayer includes the different elements that should be included in our prayers.**

You'll need—
- Bibles
- whiteboard and markers

Have a leader read Matthew 6:9-13 out loud. Let students discuss general types of prayer that Jesus modeled. Make a list of key ideas on the whiteboard. You may want to bring out any of the following elements that weren't mentioned—

- **Verse 9.** *Our Father in heaven, hallowed be your name.* Adoration, praising God for his divine characteristics.

- **Verse 10.** *Your kingdom come, your will be done on earth as it is in heaven.* Intercession, in this case, praying about the needs of the world. Jesus lined up his request with God's point of view.

- **Verse 11.** *Give us today our daily bread.* Supplication, asking God for the necessities of life.

- **Verse 12.** *Forgive us our debts, as we also have forgiven our debtors.* Confession, recalling what we've done wrong and asking God for forgiveness.

- **Verse 13.** *And lead us not into temptation, but deliver us from the evil one.* Protection, asking God to help us overcome the temptations we face.

Then talk with your team about ways to benefit from Jesus' model for prayer.

Team Prayer *20 min.*

Review—or introduce your team to—conversational prayer. Here are some key ideas you might want to share.

- *Pray! Don't talk.* If we aren't careful, a 20-minute prayer time can become 18 minutes of sharing and two minutes of praying. Rather than telling each other about the items you want the group to pray for—pray about them. If Alex is concerned about an upcoming math test, he might simply pray, "Lord, I've got this math test Friday and I am really worried about it. Please help me understand the things I need to know." Then the rest of the group will know about his concern and can also pray about it.

  - *One subject at a time.* The second key to making conversational prayer effective is to pray about only one subject at a time. If Alex prayed about his math test, then Mitch might continue on the same subject by praying, "God, I would also like to ask you to be with Alex as he takes his math test. I know how hard he has worked the last several weeks, and this upcoming test is a big part of his grade. Please help him to do well." The group would continue to pray for Alex's math test until everyone who wanted to pray for that subject had a chance to do so.

  - *Pray spontaneously.* For conversational prayer time to be the most effective, the group should pray spontaneously rather than going around the circle or in some other set order. One person might pray two or three times while someone else only prays once. Not everyone will necessarily pray about every subject. Conversational prayer is just like a conversation among friends.

  - *Keep turns short.* Prayer times, if a group is not careful, can become lengthy times of listening to someone else pray. The fourth key that makes conversational prayer different from other types of prayer is to keep the individual prayers short, so everyone is involved and energized. In normal conversation if one person talks too much it stifles the conversation. The same thing is true during prayer.

Conversational prayer takes practice and will get better as a group prays together. If your group doesn't have a lot of experience with conversational prayer, don't get discouraged if it doesn't go perfectly. For the next few weeks, review the keys to effective conversational prayer before each group prayer time.

Now, put these ideas into practice by praying. Also, keep the different elements of the Lord's Prayer in mind and try to include them.

Becoming 4 Praying Team

1. List 10 things that prevent you from praying, make it hard for you to pray, or interfere with your efforts to pray.

2. List some of the prayers God has answered for you.

3. Had any disappointments in prayer? Any prayers still unanswered? List those here.

Becoming 4 Praying Team

1. List 10 things that prevent you from praying, make it hard for you to pray, or interfere with your efforts to pray.

2. List some of the prayers God has answered for you.

3. Had any disappointments in prayer? Any prayers still unanswered? List those here.

Helping Friends in Crisis— Listening Skills

The point
Help your student leaders develop listening skills to help others in crisis.

The point, unwrapped
We've heard it a hundred times but still need to be reminded: friendship and particularly a *helping* friendship is one part talking, three parts listening. This meeting helps your students learn effective listening skills so that they can minister to their peers in crisis—and gives them a chance to first practice listening skills with other leaders before using them with friends.

Where in the Word
1 Samuel, Nehemiah, Proverbs, John, James

Team Building *10 min.*

Telephone Line
Divide your group in half and have them stand in two single-file lines about four or five feet apart. Very quietly read or tell the same story to the first person in the front of each line. The longer the story, the more interesting this activity becomes!

Each person must then whisper the story to the person behind them, being careful that the next person in line doesn't hear. When the story reaches the end of the telephone line, the last person from each line must retell the story to everyone. The whole group can then decide which line listened and communicated more clearly and effectively than the other.

Discuss these questions with your student leaders—

- **What happened to our communication in this activity?**

- **Why do you think this happened?**

- **How is this like what happens in real life when we communicate with others?**

- **How is it different?**

- **What does this activity tell us about the importance of listening carefully to others?**

You'll need—
- copies of Say What? (page 123), enough to give one card to each group
- a sheet of paper for each student
- pencils

Say What?
Divide students into groups no larger than five and give them one of the four **Say What?** cards (page 123) to discuss. Group members should briefly share their answers to the questions on the card. After about five minutes the groups exchange cards so they have

a new set of questions to discuss. As before, the group members take turns responding.

When the groups have discussed all four categories, ask each person to write down every fact they can remember from the answers that were given in their small group. Of course those with better memories are at a slight advantage, but those who really tuned in and listened (rather than concentrating on their own responses) will be able to recall the most.

Then discuss these questions—

- **Before you created your list, how well did you think you listened to the others in your group?**

- **Does your list support your opinion of your listening skills? Why or why not?**

- **How does it make you feel when you know another person is listening attentively to you?**

- **What is the importance of good listening skills to our youth ministry?**

Team Huddle *30 min.*

Direct your students along this line—

Now that we've evaluated our listening skills, we need to look into God's Word and see what listening skills he would want us to practice with him and others.

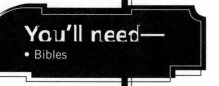

You'll need—
- Bibles

We're going to focus on several Scriptures, but in the same small groups we were just in. Each group will be assigned some Scripture to read. Discuss your individual reflections about the passage together. Then create a skit that brings out the truths expressed in your Scripture text and present it to the entire group. You'll have two minutes to perform your skit.

Assign the following passages to your groups. If you have fewer than six groups, give groups more than one reference.

1 Samuel 3:9-10	**Proverbs 18:13**
Nehemiah 8:2-3	**John 10:27**
Proverbs 12:15	**James 1:19**

Allow students about 10 minutes to study the passages and create their skits. Then have groups perform their skits.

After all the groups have presented their skits, discuss questions like these—

- **What truths did we learn about listening through the Scripture passages and our skits?**

- **How can listening in these ways help us help others, especially those in deep need?**

- **Have you ever tried any of the strategies communicated in the Bible? If so, how did they work?**

- **What's one truth you learned today that you can put into practice this week? How will you do so?**

Team Study *15 min.*

Open your discussion by saying—

> **Perhaps the most common recurring complaint of young people is, "No one ever listens to me."**

- **Do you agree or disagree with that statement? Why?**
- **What makes *you* feel like others don't listen to you?**
- **What helps you feel listened to and understood?**
- **When do you need others to listen to you the most?**
- **When is listening well to others most important?**

You'll need—
- Copies of **Do You Hear Me?** (page 124)
- pencils

Distribute **Do You Hear Me?** (page 124) and pencils. Ask students to circle their responses for the first question, then share their answers with the group. Now ask your students to rate themselves by answering the second question on the handout, then discuss their answers.

Next, review the following information about listening skills with your students. They can follow along on their handouts. Give a real-life example of each skill, and let the students share examples or thoughts they may have after each one. Explain that as students are able to master these skills, they'll be able to listen to and minister to their friends effectively.

Seven effective listening skills for students

1. **Provide an atmosphere of openness.** Give someone the opportunity to share freely by meeting one-on-one (in a private location if they're the same gender as you) and giving them your undivided attention. People don't always need to hear the right answer or have someone fix their problems for them. It's more important to establish an atmosphere of openness in which they feel you are actively listening to them. The rest of these points unpack the how-to's of active listening.

2. **Empathize.** Put yourself in her place to feel what she's feeling. Romans 12:15 applies here: "Rejoice with those who rejoice; mourn with those who mourn." If you can relate to what she's saying, you might share what you learned from your own experiences. However, keep in mind that you're supposed to be listening. Don't monopolize the conversation by trying to show her how much you can relate!

3. **Accept and validate feelings.** Let him know it's okay and normal to feel what he's feeling. Sometimes people tell others not to feel a certain way or communicate that the feelings are wrong. What's important is how to cope with the feelings.

4. **Clarify communication.** Throughout the conversation you should reflect her thoughts back to her. This is a good way to make sure you're on the right track. It can also be helpful for her to hear another perspective about her situation. You can do this by saying things like, "What I'm hearing you say is..." or "It sounds to me like you're feeling..."

5. **Use "I" messages to communicate.** Create an empathetic, nonthreatening environment by using phrases like "I feel...," "I sense...," or "I hear...," instead of "You are..." "You should...," or "You didn't..."

6. Be 100-percent present. Be aware of your nonverbal communication—eye contact, body language, posture, and so on. Sit across from him in a way that shows you're very interested in what he's saying. Lean forward with your hands in your lap or at your sides. Don't cross your arms in front of your chest—this is a closed and defensive posture. Make eye contact with him while he's speaking, but don't stare so intently that you make him feel uncomfortable. Remain relaxed, and he will too.

7. Provide reassurance of understanding. After you've talked, follow up with a phone call or another face-to-face get-together. Make a point to remember what she's told you so you can ask how things have changed or what progress she's made since you last spoke. Keeping in regular contact with her and remembering facts about her situation shows her how much you care, and it opens the door for future conversations.

You'll need—
• copies of **Do You Hear Me?** (page 124) from the last activity

Do You Hear Me?

Students should pair off and share with their partner which listening skills they possess (from the list on **Do You Hear Me?**) and which skills they need to work on. Now have those same pairs practice the listening skills with the following exercise. Review the steps before they begin; then they can refer to the handout. Let them spread out around the room to do the exercise. Give them six minutes.

Speaker: Share for three minutes about something you struggle with at school or work— or with your family or friends.

Listener: Practice using the seven skills listed above. After three minutes are up, reflect to your partner what his or her struggle is, describe what you think his or her main emotions are about the situation, and note any other significant issues.

Speaker: Give feedback to your partner. Did he or she reflect the struggle correctly? Did he or she describe your emotions accurately? Did your partner miss anything significant?

After six minutes, have students switch roles. Then, regroup and discuss the activity using some of these questions—

- **Which role—listener or speaker—was more significant to you? Why?**
- **What impact do you think listening in this way could have on people in our youth ministry?**
- **How can this kind of listening help others who are facing crises?**
- **What have you learned from this activity that you'd like to apply to your life?**

Summarize by letting them know that the art of listening takes practice. Encourage them to practice the areas they struggle with the most in day-to-day conversations.

Team Prayer 5 min.
As you close in prayer, here are few ideas for your team to pray about.

• The student leaders' skills in listening.
• Specific peers in need of listening friends.
• To be used by God as an effective listener in the lives of those specific peers.

Say What?
Your Favorites

What's your favorite time of year?

What's your favorite subject in school?

What's your favorite Bible verse?

Say What?
Your Weaknesses

What is your most annoying habit?

What do you struggle with the most spiritually?

What do wish you could do better?

Say What?
Your Grievances

What bugs you about school?

What is your least favorite vegetable?

What ticks you off?

Say What?
Your Strengths

What is your most positive personality trait?

What do you do the best?

What is your greatest spiritual strength?

Do You Hear Me?

1. Who *listens* to you? (circle your answers)

mom	counselor	friend	other _____
dad	aunt	youth pastor	no one
brother	uncle	coach	
sister	grandparent	teacher	

2. Do you see yourself as more of a listener or a talker? Rate yourself on the scale below.

●————————————————————————————————————●

listener   talker

3. Which of the following seven skills do you already have a grip on? Underline 'em. Which ones do you still need to practice? Circle those.

- Provide an atmosphere of openness.
- Empathize.
- Accept and validate feelings.
- Clarify communication.
- Use "I" messages to communicate.
- Be 100-percent present.
- Provide reassurance of understanding.

Listening Exercise

Speaker: Share for three minutes about something you struggle with at school or work—or with your family or friends.

Listener: Practice using the seven skills listed above. After three minutes are up, reflect to your partner what his or her struggle is, describe what you think his or her main emotions are about the situation, and note any other significant issues.

Speaker: Give feedback to your partner. Did he or she reflect the struggle correctly? Did he or she describe your emotions accurately? Did your partner miss anything significant?

Helping Friends in Crisis—Counseling Skills

The point
Explore tools and guidelines for counseling with your peer ministry leaders.

The point, unwrapped
As complex as counseling can be, and provided that students know when and how to refer, there's a whole lot of effective counseling a high schooler can do simply by listening well and asking a few strategic questions. With some practical and legal guidelines, and with skills that can be practiced, peer counselors can learn to respond to their friends in crisis in appropriate, healthy ways.

Where in the Word
2 Corinthians

Team Building *10 min.*

Inside Out
Pass out one Styrofoam cup and a few markers to each student. Have the students write on the outside of their cups five to 10 descriptive words of how they believe people view them (funny, emotional, outgoing, loves God). Then have them write five to 10 words that describe how they see themselves on the inside of the cup. Include both positive and negative characteristics. Let students share a few of the words from the outside and inside of their cups with the group. Then ask questions like these—

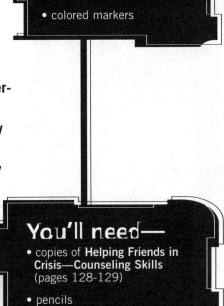

You'll need—
- Styrofoam cups
- colored markers

- **Why do you think some of the words on the inside of your cup are different from those on the outside?**

- **What does this tell you about the way you see your peers and how they see themselves?**

- **People who need help often don't appear that way on the outside. They keep the hurting part of themselves locked away. How could this activity help you recognize a person who needs help and reach out to him?**

You'll need—
- copies of **Helping Friends in Crisis—Counseling Skills** (pages 128-129)
- pencils

Team Huddle *30 min.*
Distribute **Helping Friends in Crisis—Counseling Skills** (pages 128-129) and pencils. Work through the handout with your team, using the following notes. They can and should use these tools in formal and informal counseling settings.

Steps to problem-solving

1. Identify the problem. You have to figure out what the problem is before you can move on. Ask questions to clarify. Often the presenting problem—the problem the person approaches the counselor with—is not the real problem but one designed to determine whether it's safe to talk with the counselor.

Key question: What is the main problem you're struggling with?

2. List alternative solutions. Once you've clarified the problem, help the student list (at least orally) a variety of solution options. Before the student decides on a solution, encourage her to consider the options.

Key question: What are ways you can address or respond to this problem?

3. Select a plan of action. Work up a plan that develops the selected option. Sometimes it's helpful to role-play or practice the plan. Now the process is half over.

Key question: Which alternative is the best (healthiest) choice for everyone involved?

4. Establish accountability. Almost everyone needs some form of accountability. Taking the first step can be most difficult, so follow-up is crucial. Develop a plan for accountability, too.

Key question: Who is going to follow up and walk with you during this process?

5. Set up an evaluation procedure. The counselor and the student need to evaluate the actions taken. You want to see progress, not necessarily perfection. Consider using regular phone calls, checkup meetings, or keeping a journal.

Key question: How and when are we going to evaluate your progress?

Reporting Requirements

Peer counselors may be subject to the same state laws that professional counselors and youth workers must follow—to report physical or sexual abuse and certain other dangers to the authorities, often within a specific time limit.

Know your state laws about reporting requirements and communicate them to your peer counselors.

Be sure your student leaders understand that they're to discuss reportable situations *only* with appropriate adults (you would usually be one of them), but not with other students or uninvolved adults. Also, advise your peer counselors about how to follow up with the at-risk student.

Probing questions

Whenever peer counselors don't know the *real* issue their friends are dealing with, or how to clarify or resolve the problem, they can ask these questions to probe further. Questions like these—and time—can often help ferret out the actual problem, cutting through mere surface details. Peer counselors should memorize these three questions.

- *What do you want to receive [or understand or know]?*
- *How are you feeling?* [Accept and validate these right away.]
- *What are you going to do about the problem?*

Confidentiality

- **Trust.** When people choose to confide in you, they're trusting you with their confidence. Only if confidentiality is practiced can trust be established.

- **Credibility.** If you break a student's confidence, you've not only hurt your credibility with her, but also damaged a relationship. And news about your indiscretion will travel quickly to the rest of the school, youth group, or church (depending on where your connection is with this student).

- **Limitations and boundaries.** Consider this the golden rule of confidentiality: *Do not break any confidences to other friends, students, teachers, counselors, parents, or youth leaders—unless students or others are endangered.*

Talkback

After you've discussed the above principles, make sure you give your student leaders opportunities to ask questions about counseling their friends in crisis. This could be the most crucial part of your peer ministry training. If you don't have an answer for any question, get it for your student as soon as possible. Your wise and quick response is crucial—it could affect lives if a friend is suicidal.

Counseling Role-Play

A good way to prepare your students for real life is to practice through role-plays. Invite a pair of students to the front and explain a crisis scenario. One student leader can play the role of the peer counselor and the other can be the friend in crisis. Let them play the roles—incorporating the steps and questions presented during this session—while the rest of the group observes. Here are some scenarios:

- The student's parents are getting a divorce.
- The student is failing classes in school.
- The student is pregnant.
- The student is addicted to a street drug.
- The student is suicidal.
- The student's girlfriend just broke up with him.
- The student's boyfriend is pressuring her to have sex.
- The student is being sexually molested by an uncle.
- The student's parent is an alcoholic and abuses the student.
- The student is struggling with his sexual identity and is experimenting.

> ## You'll need—
> - copies of **Helping Friends in Crisis—Counseling Skills** (pages 128-129) from the last activity
> - Bibles
> - pencils

Afterward, discuss the role-plays. Give the role-playing students the opportunity to share what they might have said differently. Encourage observers to point out what the students did well and what they might have done differently. Invite students to ask questions. Answer what you can and report back on questions you have to research.

Team Study *10 min.*

Have students team up with their partners to go through the **"Team Study"** portion of **Helping Friends in Crisis—Counseling Skills** (pages 128-129). Then gather the group together. Read 2 Corinthians 4:7 and continue with comments along these lines—

You are a jar of clay. You hold a treasure within you that has the power to minister healing, wholeness, hope, love, comfort, and safety to your friends in crisis. This treasure was given to you only so you could to give it away to those in need. So look around you, see who is in need, then share with them the treasure you've received.

Team Prayer *10 min.*

In small groups, have the students answer the first question below, pray for each other, answer the second question, then pray for their friends.

1. In what area of your life do you need to receive comfort from God right now (family, school, friendships, other relationships)?
2. Who do you know who needs comforting that you can give (friend, family member)? What does he need?

Helping Friends in Crisis—
Counseling Skills

Steps to problem-solving

1. Identify the problem.
Key question: What is the main problem you're struggling with?

2. List alternative solutions.
Key question: What are ways you can address or respond to this problem?

3. Select a plan of action.
Key question: Which alternative is the best or healthiest choice for everyone involved?

4. Establish and enforce accountability.
Key question: Who is going to walk with you through this process?

5. Set up an evaluation procedure.
Key question: How and when are we going to evaluate your progress?

Probing questions
Ask one or more of these questions if you get stuck:

• *What do you want to receive [or understand or know]?*

• *How are you feeling?* [Accept and validate these feelings right away.]

• *What are you going to do about the problem?* [The decision is ultimately your friend's.]

(continued)

(Helping Friends in Crisis—Counseling Skills, p. 2)

Confidentiality

• Trust

• Credibility

• Limitations and boundaries

Team Study

In your small groups read 2 Corinthians 1:3-11 and discuss the following questions.

• What do you observe in this Bible passage about comforting others?

• What do you think about how God comforted Paul and Timothy?

• What does this passage tell you about your resources for serving others who have problems?

• How have you received comfort from God recently in your life?

• Have you been able to comfort someone else because of the comfort you received? Tell about it.

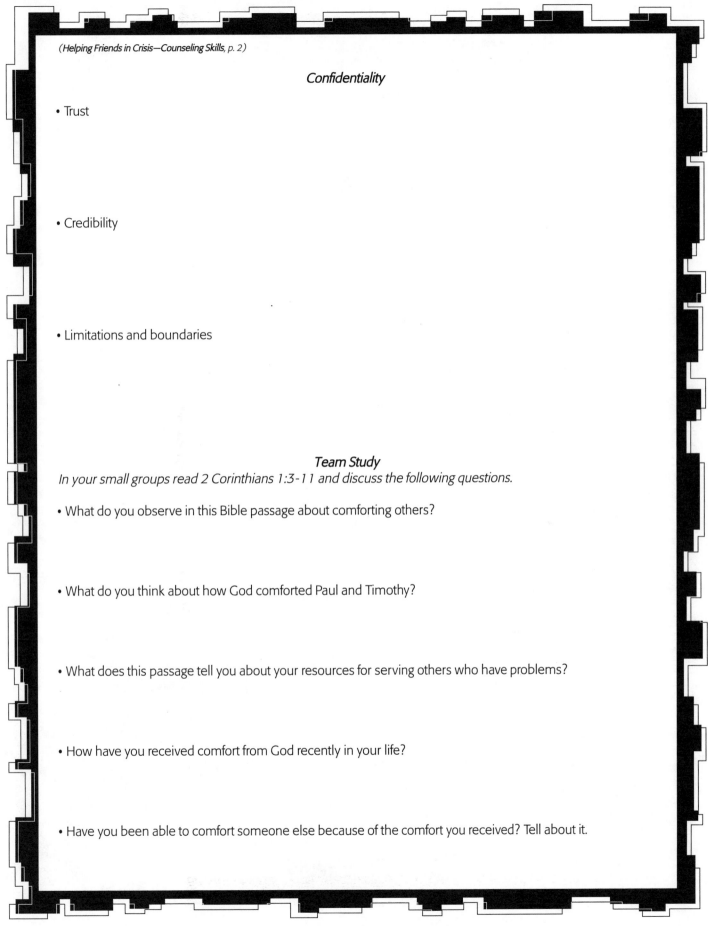

From *Student Leadership Training Manual* by Dennis "Tiger" McLuen & Chuck Wysong. Permission to reproduce this page granted only for use in the buyer's own youth group. www.YouthSpecialties.com

129

Helping Friends in Crisis— Case Studies

The point
Practicing counseling skills.

The point, unwrapped
The format of this session is noticeably different from the other two **Helping Friends in Crisis** sessions. Spend time reviewing the important points from those two sessions, and make sure your students understand them well. Answer any questions that may have come up since you first introduced the material.

Seven effective listening skills for students

1. Provide an atmosphere of openness.

2. Empathize.

3. Accept and validate feelings.

4. Clarify communication.

5. Use "I" messages to communicate.

6. Be 100-percent present.

7. Provide reassurance of understanding.

Steps to problem solving

1. Identify the problem.
   Key question: What is the main problem you're struggling with?

2. List alternative solutions.
   Key question: What are ways you can address or respond to this problem?

3. Select a plan of action.
   Key question: Which alternative is the best or healthiest choice for everyone involved?

4. Establish and enforce accountability.
   Key question: Who is going to walk with you through this process?

5. Set up an evaluation procedure.
   Key question: How and when are we going to evaluate your progress?

Probing questions

- *What do you want to receive [or understand or know]?*
- *How are you feeling?* [Accept and validate these feelings right away.]
- *What are you going to do about the problem?* [The decision is ultimately your friend's.]

Confidentiality

- Trust
- Credibility
- Limitations and boundaries

You'll need—

- three student actors (optional)
- copies of **Tanisha and Cole—Case Studies** (page 133) for the actors
- copies of **Tanisha and Cole—Questions** (page 134) for your student leaders
- pencils
- whiteboard and markers

Some of your students may see suicidal tendencies in Cole—his withdrawing into his room for much of the day, his perceived lack of options, his remark to Kaylee that he "couldn't take it anymore." If the subject comes up, impress on your student leaders that *whenever they suspect that a peer is suicidal, they should immediately contact a responsible adult or agency.* The life of at least that peer—and perhaps other lives—is at stake.

Case Studies

Recruit three students (you may know of some gifted actors who aren't necessarily part of the peer ministry) to role-play the characters in this lesson's case studies. Give the actors **Tanisha and Cole—Case Studies** (page 133) ahead of time to use as a guide for acting out the scenarios. Tanisha can talk to the student leaders in a monologue as if she's talking with a friend. Cole and Kaylee can talk with each other and let the student leaders observe the dialogue. (You can just read each case study to the group if you need to.)

After the first scenario, give your student leaders the opportunity to ask questions. Your actors should respond to the questions as if they were the characters Then distribute copies of **Tanisha and Cole—Questions** (page 134) and pencils. Let your team members work individually or in small groups to answer the questions on their handout for the first case study. After a few minutes, discuss the answers all together. Compile responses to the questions on a whiteboard.

Repeat the process with the second case study.

Team Prayer

Let the students get into groups of two or three to pray. Pray that God will guide them while they listen to and advise their peers. And pray that he will remind them of all that they've learned about counseling others during these three sessions when they need to remember it.

Tanisha and Cole
CASE STUDIES

Tanisha

Tanisha is a sophomore in high school. She's an average student academically, but she loves music. She has a powerful voice and sings in a local band that plays at coffeehouses, school dances, and some parties. She hardly has any friends outside the band—the other musicians are her closest friends. Tanisha loves to sing on stage. It's like an escape for her. She spends most of her time practicing with the band or just hanging out.

She's rarely at home, and whenever she is there she's called a "no-good low-life who isn't going to get anywhere in life unless you study more, get better grades, and get a college education."

What Tanisha's parents don't know is that she wants to go to a music school, focus on her music, and start recording with her band. They never ask about her future plans, nor do they seem to care. Tanisha feels like the only people who care about her are her friends from the band, but even they mostly talk about their music and upcoming schedule of gigs.

Tanisha's begun to doubt that she'll ever make it big—even if she's really good enough or has the drive to go for it.

Cole

Cole lives down the street from Kaylee. He's very shy and quiet and only has a few friends. One of them is Kaylee. He likes hanging around with her because she's funny, she's energetic, and she's always there for him.

Cole's parents divorced when he was three years old. He lives with his mom, who drinks a lot; and he hasn't really seen his dad since the divorce. Cole doesn't like being home at night because that's when his mom gets really loaded. So he hangs out at Kaylee's.

One night Cole told Kaylee that he'd been skipping school because he was tired a lot. During the day he just stays in his room, listens to music, and writes poems. Cole told her that his mom went crazy last night, tore up the house, screamed, and threw things everywhere. Her drinking had gotten much worse. Cole hadn't spoken to his mom in weeks, and he couldn't take it anymore. He said he couldn't move out because his mom couldn't handle that, but he couldn't stay there either.

Cole wanted to thank Kaylee for being there for him whenever he needed her and gave his book of poems to her. He wanted her to have the thing that matters most to him, because she's the most important person in his life.

Tanisha & Cole Questions

Tanisha

1. What feelings do you think Tanisha is experiencing?

2. If Tanisha came to you as a friend, how would you encourage her? What would you say to her? What Scriptures could you share with her?

3. If Jesus sat down with her, what might he tell Tanisha? How does that contrast with the actions and words of Tanisha's parents?

4. What feedback could you give to Tanisha that would help her move toward a healthier view of herself and God's plan for her life?

Cole

1 What signs do you see that Cole might try to attempt suicide? Talk about them.

2. How would you respond if you were Kaylee?

3. What action steps could Kaylee take to prevent Cole from committing suicide?

4. How could Kaylee continue to be a friend to Cole and walk with him through this rough time in his life?

Developing a Heart for Lost People

The point
Cultivating a heart for those who don't know Christ.

The point, unwrapped
In this session your student leaders explore the heart and motives of the apostle Paul, one of Christianity's first and greatest evangelists—and in particular, four motives that can empower teenagers to share the gospel with their friends.

Where in the Word
Luke, 2 Corinthians, Acts

Team Building *15 min.*

The Message Game
Tell students that you want them to get to know each other better. Pair up students and give each a copy of **Ten Facts** (page 139) and a pencil. When you give the signal, students have two minutes for one partner to fill out the fact sheet. Teens switch roles for the last two minutes.

Appear ready to begin, but hesitate—and have students move 10 feet apart. Again, look like you're ready to give the signal, but turn on the CD with the volume as loud as you can tolerate.

After four minutes (you may want to give a half-way warning), turn off the music and bring students together to discuss some of the following questions. You can jot key words on a whiteboard, so you can refer to them as you continue your discussion.

- **What's your reaction to this activity?**

- **Did you find anything frustrating about communicating with each other during this activity? If so, what made you frustrated?**

- **Let's list the obstacles we had to overcome to communicate with each other.**

- **How was this activity like trying to share your faith with others? How is it different?**

- **What obstacles stand between you and non-Christians you know?**

- **What fears hold you back from sharing the gospel with them?**

You'll need—
- copies of **Ten Facts** (page 139)
- pencils
- whiteboard and marker (optional)
- CD (of music that rocks!)
- CD player

Team Huddle *15 min.*

Now, turn your students' attention to the following story.

The Lifesaving Station

On a dangerous seacoast where shipwrecks often occur, there was once a crude little lifesaving station. The building was just a hut, and there was only one boat, but the few devoted members kept a constant watch over the sea and, with no thought for themselves, went out day and night tirelessly searching for the lost. Some of those who were saved, and various others in the surrounding area, wanted to become associated with the station and give of their time, money, and effort for the support of the work. New boats were bought and new crews trained. The little lifesaving station grew.

Some of the members of the lifesaving stations were unhappy that the building was so crude and poorly equipped. They felt that a more comfortable place should be provided as the first refuge of those saved from the sea. They replaced the emergency cots with beds and put better furniture in the enlarged building. The newly decorated and exquisitely furnished lifesaving station became a popular gathering place for its members, a sort of clubhouse. Fewer members were now interested in going to sea on lifesaving missions, so they hired lifeboat crews to do this work. The lifesaving motif still prevailed in the club's decoration, however, and there was a liturgical lifeboat in the room where the club initiations were held.

From *Hot Illustrations for Youth Talks* by Wayne Rice, Youth Specialties, 1994.

About this time a large ship was wrecked off the coast, and the hired crews brought in the boatloads of cold, wet, and half-drowned people. They were dirty and sick, and some of them had black skin and some had yellow skin. They dripped on the rug and water-stained the furniture in the beautiful new club. So the property committee immediately had a shower house built outside the club where victims of shipwreck could be cleaned up before coming inside.

At the next meeting, there was a split in the club membership. Most of the members wanted to stop the club's lifesaving activities as being unpleasant and a hindrance to the normal social life of the club. Some members insisted upon lifesaving as their primary purpose and pointed out that they were still called a lifesaving station. But they were finally voted down and told that if they wanted to save the lives of all the various kinds of people who were shipwrecked in those waters, they could begin their own lifesaving station down the coast. They did.

As the years went by, the new station experienced the same changes that had occurred in the old. It evolved into a club, and yet another lifesaving station was founded. History continued to repeat itself, and if you visit that seacoast today, you will find a number of exclusive clubs along that shore. Shipwrecks are frequent in those waters, but most of the people drown.

After reading the story, analyze the story by asking your team questions like these—

- **When was the lifesaving station most effective? When was it least effective?**

- **How are the attitudes of the station's members like that of the church? How are they different?**

- **What can we learn about our purposes as a leadership team from this story?**

Explain that sometimes our attitudes are the biggest obstacle to sharing our faith with others. To overcome that obstacle, and any others that block our way, we need to allow God to cultivate a heart in us for those who don't know him yet.

Team Study 20 min.

To begin, you might say—

> **In the Bible, God never gives a command without providing the proper motivation to spur us on to obedience. And when it comes to sharing the gospel, this is definitely the case. Let's look at some Bible verses about our motivation for sharing the Good News.**

You'll need—
- copies of **Developing a Heart for Lost People** (page 139)
- Bibles
- pencils

Hand out copies of **Developing a Heart for Lost People** (page 139) and pencils. Let your team leaders read 2 Corinthians 5:11-21 and list 10 observations from the passage on the handout—especially motivations they might notice. After a few minutes, come together and share observations.

Let students jot down these four motivations as you review the following ideas with them. Cover these points in your own words and in as much depth as time allows.

The fear of the Lord (verse 11). Possible directions to take the discussion:

- **What exactly is "the fear of the Lord"?**

- **How can fear be a good thing?**

- **What is the relationship between "the fear of the Lord" and reaching out to friends who need Jesus?**

The love of Christ (verses 13-15). Relevant Bible passages you may want to use: Romans 14:7-9, Galatians 2:20-21, 1 Peter 4:1-5. Possible directions to take the discussion:

- **How does a friend's or relative's love motivate you?**

- **When that love for you is expressed in outright sacrifice, how does that make you feel? Under obligation? Grateful? Cared for?**

- **What do you feel when you think of (1) Christ's sacrifice for you, and (2) the need of your friends for God?**

A new start (verses 16-17). Possible directions to take the discussion:

- **If those "in Christ" are new creations, what's old about those not in Christ?**

- **In what ways is a Christian "new"?**

- **In a Christian, what exactly is the "old"? And in what sense is it "gone"?**

The calling and responsibility of an ambassador (verses 18-21). Relevant Bible passages you may want to use: Acts 10:39-43, 1 Timothy 2:1-7. Possible directions to take the discussion:

- An ambassador officially represents her nation (or organization or boss). It's through an ambassador that her nation (or organization or boss) communicates with another, more distant power. In our case, we are ambassadors representing Christ, whose message is reconciliation—and the delivery of that message from Christ to the world depends on us.

- If an ambassador is to be an effective representative of his own (distant) government, he must know and be comfortable with the language and the culture of the nation he is an ambassador to. What does this mean for us as Christ's ambassadors?

- In the 2 Corinthians verses, note the urgency of Paul's language in words like appeal and implore. Much of an ambassador's job is to appeal and implore. As Christ's ambassadors, what appeal do we make? To whom do we appeal? Who do we implore—and why?

Ask students to star one motivation on their sheets that compels them the most. Have them underline the one they feel God needs to increase in their life. If you want, take a few minutes so students can share and discuss their choices.

Have your student leaders write down their "Five Most Wanted," a list of pre-Christian students they most want to see in heaven with them.

Team Prayer *15 min.*

End this session on your knees. Encourage students to pray for—

- God to make the motivations a reality for the student leaders and other students involved with the youth group.
- The students on the "Five Most Wanted" lists.

Developing a Heart for Lost People

1. List 10 observations from 2 Corinthians 5:1-21 (especially motivations for sharing the gospel with others).

• • • • •

• • • • •

2. Jot down notes about the motivations for sharing his faith that Paul mentions .

3. List your Five Most Wanted (five pre-Christian students you'd most like to see in heaven someday).

• • • • •

Ten Facts

Find out these facts about your partner.

Favorite dessert

Dream job

Favorite movie

Least favorite subject in school

Favorite sports team

Birthplace

Favorite holiday

Worst nightmare

Favorite Bible story or verse

Most desirable place to visit or live

Sharing Your Faith with Your Friends

The point

Each leader has a unique style of sharing the Good News with others.

The point, unwrapped

In the previous session, we looked at *motivations* for sharing the gospel with friends. This session examines the *personal styles* in which high schoolers can share the gospel. The knack is uncovering how God has uniquely gifted and empowered you to share the gospel—then sharing it in a way that is uniquely yours. For while the message of the gospel never changes, the style and approach with which it's shared is as varied in a student ministry as the students themselves.

Where in the Word

John, Acts

Team Building *10 min.*

Triangle Tag

As students enter the room for the meeting, mark the backs of their hands with a colored marker—or, if you have only one marker, with a distinctive figure—so that there are four students of each color (or figure). When you're ready to begin, tell your students to find their foursome, then arrange themselves like this: one student stands in the center, and the remaining three hold hands and form a triangle around her.

Now select one of the foursomes as "It," composed of the Evangelist (the center student) and his three surrounding "triangle" students. Blindfold the Evangelist.

Meanwhile, in all the other foursomes, the students forming the triangles should face out. This helps distinguish the tagged teams from the untagged teams.

The Evangelist now has five minutes to tag other center students. He cannot move outside his triangle, and he must tag *center students*, not merely members of other triangles.

The other triangles, of course, careen their center students around the room to avoid being tagged by the Evangelist. When they're finally tagged, however, the triangle students reform, facing *in* now, the center student gets blindfolded, and this foursome now joins forces with the Evangelist in tagging others.

The game ends when either all of the center students have been tagged—that is, when all triangle students of all foursomes are facing inward—or when five minutes is up.

Have the students come together as a group and debrief the Triangle Tag game. Ask them—

- **What's your reaction to this game?**

- **How did the triangles help or hinder the tagging process?**

- **How did the Evangelist—and later, the tagged center students—feel while playing blindfolded? Were the triangles more helpful when center students became blindfolded?**

Leader hint—

This session assumes that your students have a working knowledge of the gospel. If you have students who don't have a particularly strong grasp of this, but are otherwise leadership students, such students may want to use any one of a jillion kinds of tracts that summarizes the basics in a variety of ways. See some at your Christian bookstore, or check out some Web sites, these among them:

- www.tracts.com

- www.godssimpleplan.org/gsps.html

- www.free-gifts.com

For more extended training on evangelism, see *Live the Life! Student Evangelism Training Kit* (Youth Specialties, 1998).

You'll need—

- At least 12 students

- Markers of several different colors

- Blindfolds, one for every four students

If your group is smaller than 12, use the **Confidential Arithmetic** activity on (page 142)

• As more people were tagged, was it easier or more difficult to reach the untagged?

• What did having a time limit do for the tagging process?

• Any similarities you notice between this goofy tag game and the task of reaching others for Christ? Any differences?

Confidential Arithmetic

Ask each student to think of a number between one and seven—and keep it to themselves. Ask them to double it, add 10, divide it in half, and then subtract their original number.

The answer, always and regardless of the number they originally chose: five. Follow this with words to this effect:

> **The number you originally picked may have been your birth month, it may have been a lucky number for you, or maybe you just settled on a number at random. At any rate, the number you chose, you chose for your own reasons—or for no reason. However personal that choice was, the answer for everyone was five.**
>
> **It's a little like how God uses us in evangelism. In the task of reaching your friends for Jesus Christ, you start with your own personality, your own abilities, your own weaknesses, your own gifts—yet the goal is the same goal for all of us: the addition of our friends to the body of Christ.**
>
> **Let's explore how we can do that—first of all, by looking at seven different styles of evangelism found in the New Testament.**

Team Study *20 min.*

If you like to display visuals for your students, make a transparency of **Seven Styles of Evangelism** (page 144) and place it on the overhead projector. Hand out paper copies of **Seven Styles of Evangelism** and pencils. You can also just talk through the handout with your student leaders if you prefer.

Work through the styles of evangelism by having volunteers read the Bible passages aloud and letting students make observations. You can write key words in the fourth column on the transparency.

Here are some additional notes that you can share with your students.

• **Andrew.** Andrew was one of the first disciples. He'd studied with John the Baptist, and he believed what John said about the coming Messiah, so he was eager to follow Jesus after meeting him for the very first time. After he spent most of the day with Jesus, he went to tell his brother Peter about him. Sharing Christ with those we're in a relationship with is one of the most effective means of evangelism.

• **The woman at the well.** When she met Jesus for the first time, the woman at the well had at least two strikes against her:
  ✿ She was a member of a mixed ethnic group (Samaritans) despised by the Jews.
  ✿ Even among her own villagers, she had a dubious moral reputation (and Jesus was aware of it by her midday appearance at the well).
Which is why a typical Jewish man wouldn't stop to talk to her. But Jesus wasn't typical. His actions showed that the gospel is good news for everyone—no matter what ethnic background, social status, or personal history.

You'll need—

• overhead projector and marker (optional)

• a transparency of **Seven Styles of Evangelism** (page 144) and copies for your students

• Bibles

• pencils

Adapted from *Becoming a Contagious Christian* by Bill Hybels and Mark Mittleberg (Zondervan, 1994). Used by permission.

This woman immediately told others about what Jesus had shared with her. Then she invited the whole town to come and meet him! A modern parallel might be inviting friends to an evangelistic event.

Many from the village came to hear Jesus that day, in spite of the reputation of the messenger. Perhaps they noticed that something was new and different about her. Don't let your past or reputation—or that of other people—keep you from sharing the gospel.

• **The blind man.** This man didn't know how he was healed, but he knew *who* healed him—and he wasn't afraid to tell the truth. In fact, he was brave enough to give his testimony to some high-powered religious leaders—some intimidating guys! He told them all about the difference Jesus had made in his life.

Everyone has a God story—an account of the difference Jesus made in his life. God wants to use that story in others' lives. We don't have to know all the answers—we only need to tell what Jesus has done for us.

• **Peter.** The crowd didn't intimidate Peter. He stood up and preached a fantastic evangelistic sermon with God-sized results. This style is not for everyone, but God has gifted some to lead others to Christ this way. As the Bible shows us over and over again, God likes to work through the most unlikely people! Billy Graham is a modern example of this type of evangelist.

• **Philip.** In obedience to the Holy Spirit, and without waiting, he took the initiative with the Ethiopian. Philip began the conversation by noting what the man was reading. We can begin our evangelistic conversations by noting their interests and concerns, and then shining the light of the gospel on those issues.

Analyzing these styles of evangelism may uncover areas of further interest your students may have—how to answer questions their friends may raise, how to share their testimonies, the need for social action, public speaking. Be sensitive to these needs, and consider spending additional time addressing them.

• **Tabitha.** This woman of faith was always doing good and serving others, especially the poor. When she died many people were saddened. Even people who feel like they can't speak effectively with others about God's love can *show* them his love through actions and godly character. The proverb "actions speak louder than words" is true. Many people have been won over when they experience God's love through another person. Mother Teresa is an example of this type of evangelist.

• **Paul.** Paul engaged intellectual Greeks with the kind of incisive arguments and persuasive logic they could relate to. The point? Somehow establish what you have in common with listeners before helping them follow Jesus. Josh McDowell is a modern example of this type of evangelist.

After reviewing the styles of evangelism, ask some of these questions—

- **In what situations might each of these styles be most appropriate?**
- **Which of these styles seems most comfortable to you?**
- **How might God want you to use that style this week?**

Team Prayer *15 min.*
End your session in prayer. Consider these ideas—

• Thank God for creating different styles of evangelism.
• Ask God to enable students to share the gospel in ways consistent with how God created them.
• Pray for the Five Most Wanted, from Session 18.

If you're planning an outreach event, pray for it, too.

Seven Styles of Evangelism

Evangelism Style	Biblical figure who used this style	Where you can read about this person	Notes
Relational	Andrew	John 1:35-42	
Invitation	Woman at the well	John 4:4-30, 39	
Story	The blind man	John 9:8-13, 17-27	
Proclamation	Peter	Acts 2:14, 22-24, 33, 36-41	
Initiative	Philip	Acts 8:26-38	
Service	Tabitha	Acts 9:36-42	
Intellectual	Paul	Acts 17:22-34	

Equipping Students for On-Campus Ministries

The point
You can influence others for Christ not only in youth group, but also on campus.

The point, unwrapped
Since school is a primary location for student leaders' ministry, there are several methods by which student leaders can implement ministries on their own campuses.

Where in the Word
Esther, Hosea, Ephesians

Team Building *10 min.*

What's the Use?
Divide your students into small groups of four or five. Give each group a paper bag full of items. The groups must rename each item and determine its new use. For example, a spoon may become a hand-held M&M launcher. Have each group come up with a short skit demonstrating the new names and uses for all the items in the bags. All students should have parts in the skits.

Debrief this activity by saying something like—

We usually look at familiar items and think of using them in just one way, but consider all the creative, alternative uses that you came up with for these familiar items. Just as you developed fresh, new uses for these items, God can use you in fresh, new ways to reach the world for Christ. We're going to think more about reaching your campuses for Christ during today's lesson.

You'll need—
- one paper bag for every four or five students, containing several everyday items (a spoon, salt shaker, old sock, toothpick, cotton swab)

Team Huddle *15 min.*
Pass out pencils and **Equipping Students for On-Campus Ministry** (pages 148-149). Ask the students to pair off—with another student from the same school, if possible—and answer the questions under **"Your School."** When they've finished that section, you could say—

Many students and adults have been led to believe that Christians have virtually no right to even talk about their religious beliefs on campus. Let's take a short quiz to see what you know about your religious rights on campus.

You'll need—
- copies of **Equipping Students for On-Campus Ministry** (pages 148-149)
- pencils

Now have them take the quiz under **"Your Rights"** on the handout. Here are the answers:

1. **True.** Literature may not be restricted simply because it's religious.
2. **False.** Students have the right to be exempted from activities and class content that contradicts their religious beliefs.
3. **False.** Students have the right to pray on campus as long as it's not disruptive and others are not forced to participate.
4. **True.** Only school-directed Bible reading is considered unconstitutional.

The Equal Access Act provides religious groups the same opportunities that all other noncurricular groups have on campus. Read the Equal Access Act in the United States Constitution (20 U.S.C. 4071-4074). For more information look around on the Internet or contact the American Center for Law and Justice, P.O. Box 64429, Virginia Beach, VA 23467.

You'll need—
- copies of **Equipping Students for On-Campus Ministry** (pages 148-149) from the last activity
- Bibles
- pencils

Challenge your students to begin thinking about ministry on their campus from a totally different perspective by saying something like—

You have the right to _be_ a Christian and talk about your faith with your friends on your campus.

Team Study 10 min.

Introduce the study by reminding them of their strategic place in their school. Say something like—

There are some things that adult youth workers just can't accomplish as well as students can, and one of those is reaching your friends at school for Jesus Christ. Sure, we can get to know your teachers and principals and even attend a few of your events on campus so people may know who we are. But there's nobody else in the world who can impact your friends' lives like you! After all, you've spent lots of time building relationships with your non-Christian friends at school, and they respect you because of your friendship.

Divide the students into three teams and assign each group one of the Bible passages listed under **"Your Ministry"** on the handout. After they read and discuss their part, ask each group to report their findings.

Move on to **"Your Response."** Some ideas for impacting the campus are given there (and below, with some additional explanation). Have students brainstorm additional ideas for how they can show God's love on their campus. To generate the most creative ideas, ask students not to critique the viability of ideas during the brainstorming time. Often one zany idea leads to another and another. The truly great idea is often spawned from mediocre ones. Evaluate them at another time.

- **Listen to your friends.** Whenever your friends come to you with problems or concerns you have an awesome opportunity to point them to Jesus in a natural and loving way.
- **Offer free tutoring.** Grades are important. Build relationships by helping friends with their difficult subject areas.
- **Loan out Christian CDs or books.** Circulate a good Christian CD or book among your friends.
- **Wash windshields in the parking lot.** Clean windshields in the school parking lot and leave an encouraging note, perhaps with an inspirational Bible verse.
- **Deliver donuts and coffee to the teachers' lounge.** Most teachers are dedicated and work hard. They're encouraged when students express appreciation. Turn it into a birthday club by honoring teachers on their birthdays with refreshments and a card.

- **Organize a sports outreach.** You can organize a preseason spaghetti dinner for the team, including a short program that features a testimony given by a pro athlete. (You can find these type of videos through Navigators, Youth for Christ, Athletes in Action, or similar groups.) You can also provide refreshments for the team during a practice break, and perhaps sharing your testimony.

- **Give away candy bars.** With appropriate administrative approval, hand out candy bars as students arrive at school in the morning. Attach an encouraging Bible verse printed on a small card. You can also give away bagels, Pop-Tarts, soda, pencils, or other small items.

Conclude this section by saying something like—

> **There are many ways to reach your unsaved friends at school for Jesus Christ. You just have to realize that deep down inside, all of your friends *do* want to know God intimately. Because of the relationship you have built with them over the years, many of your friends—who would never set foot inside a church—would be happy to listen to what you have to say about Christ.**
>
> **The most important ingredient to remember when sharing with your friends is love. God loves you, and it's important for you to show your friends that God loves them in the same way! It may not happen instantaneously, but as your friends see you living out a loving, positive example of Christ's love at school, they'll want what you have!**

Close the session by having each student share one ministry they'll try to initiate on their campus and when they'll do it.

Team Prayer *20 min.*

Finish up by praying in small groups for some of these ideas—

- For God's help and guidance as student leaders pursue their new ideas for ministering to their schoolmates.
- For God to develop within each student leader a deep love and passion for lost students on campus.
- For God to lead them to other students on campus who may share the same evangelistic vision.
- For student leaders to be willing to be used by God.

Equipping Students for On-Campus Ministry

Your school

1. What ministries are on your school campus? (like Fellowship of Christian Athletes, Young Life, Campus Life, campus Christian club, See You at the Pole, none, etc.). What do they do, or what is their purpose?

2. If you have friends that don't go to the events these groups sponsor, why don't they go?

3. What faculty members (administrators, counselors, coaches, etc.) may be Christians, do you think?

Your rights

Take this short quiz about student's legal rights.

True   False   **1.** Students have the right to express their religious beliefs by distributing religious literature on campus.

True   False   **2.** Students must attend a required class even if it contradicts their religious beliefs.

True   False   **3.** Students may not pray on public school campuses.

True   False   **4.** Students may carry and read their Bible on campus.

Your ministry

Read the verses and answer the questions.

Esther 4:12-14

• Put in your own words what God was telling Esther through Mordecai.

• How does this truth apply to you and your ministry at school?

• How do you want to respond?

(continued)

Hosea 4:5-6

• Summarize what God was trying to tell Israel through Hosea.

• Why is it important for students to know their rights as Christians on public school campuses?

• How do you want to respond?

Ephesians 4:11-13

• What are *works of service*?

• What are some of the best ways that youth workers can prepare students to serve in their schools?

• What are the reasons for preparing to serve? State them in your own words.

• How can your youth leaders help you reach these goals?

Your response
*Brainstorm some practical ways you can show God's love to your friends and your school.
Here are a few to get you going—*

Listen to your friends

Deliver donuts and coffee to the teachers' lounge

Offer free tutoring

Organize a sports outreach

Loan out Christian CDs or books

Give away candy bars

Wash windshields in the parking lot

How to start a student-led prayer group at your school

1. **Connect with other Christians at your school.** Tell other Christian students in your youth group or para-church group (Fellowship of Christian Athletes, Young Life, Campus Life, etc.) about your desire to start a prayer group at school, and ask if they want to join you. Pray off-campus for your school until you have approval to meet on campus.

2. **Get a faculty sponsor.** Your school may require it—but even if they don't, it's good to have an adult around for encouragement and advice. Ask around until you've identified a Christian teacher who you think would be a good advisor, then go talk to her—but not before you've put in writing, clearly and specifically, what you want her to do and not do. At the top of your request list will probably be the use of her classroom to pray in.

3. **Know the law.** Your school has policies about curricular and extracurricular groups meeting on campus. And you have certain rights under the federal Equal Access Act. Unless you know your school's administration is very favorable to the idea of a prayer group on campus, you'd be wise to brush up on just what the EAA says and what your local policies are—before you meet with the administration (below). Maybe your faculty sponsor will help you here. The text of the Equal Access Act and other helpful information is available on the Internet. Generally speaking, if your school allows other noncurricular groups to meet on campus, you also have the right to meet for prayer.

4. **Ask the appropriate administrator about starting the group.** Explain to the principal or VP what you want to do, about how many students will be involved, who your faculty sponsor is, when and where you want to meet, and other pertinent information. Explain whether you're seeking club status or whether you just want to meet to pray.
   If the administrator denies your request, don't get hostile or argumentative. Rather, explain what you understand the Equal Access Act means for prayer groups on your campus. If you still do not receive permission, wait a few weeks, pray for God to open the door, and gather signatures of students who will come to the prayer meetings and of teachers who

support you. Give this list to your principal and ask for your plan to be reconsidered. If the principal still say no, consider taking the issue to your school board.

5. **Finalize the time and day to meet.** Once you've got administrative approval, select a time and day that works for the most people. Consider meeting in the morning—it's a great way to start the day, and you're more likely to attract students whose purpose is to pray rather than socialize or let off steam (which are natural after-school tendencies).

6. **Spread the word.** Promote the prayer meeting with fliers and by word of mouth. Ask youth workers of churches in your area to announce the prayer meeting to their youth groups.

7. **The first meeting**
   - Share the reason the prayer group is being started.
   - Form an informal leadership team (for planning extra events).
   - Pray!

Other suggestions

- Interest levels will stay higher if you vary the order of each meeting, instead of following the same routine each week.
- Divide into pairs, into groups of three or four, or (if your group is on the small side) stay in one group. From week to week, suggest that students change the groupings in which they pray.
- Maybe set up chairs in small circles around the room. At each station, have specific or general prayer ideas. Let small groups rotate among the stations.
- Pray for personal needs, upcoming events, non-Christian students, teachers, administrators, staff, opportunities to share the gospel. And take time to focus on praise and thanksgiving.
- Pray through Bible passages about prayer (Ephesians 1:17-20, Colossians 1:9-12, 1 Thessalonians 3:12-13, etc.). Insert the names of student into the text.
- Be creative!
- Sample agenda for a campus prayer meeting:
  ◎ Announce a specific prayer focus for the day (topic in the news, a Bible verse, thanksgiving, etc.).
  ◎ Divide into groups of four or five (mix it up—this builds unity and makes newcomers feel welcome).
  ◎ Give each group a teacher to pray for.
  ◎ Pray.

—Joel Newton, Ft. Wayne, Ind., Youth for Christ

The Plan behind Your Prayers

The point
Prayer prepares people for meeting Jesus.

The point, unwrapped
The aim of this session is to equip your student leaders to pray knowledgeably and evangelistically for friends, classmates, and family members who need Jesus.

Where in the Word
Luke, Acts, Romans, Ephesians, Colossians, 1 Timothy, Hebrews, 1 John

Team Building *20 min.*

The Search
Before your meeting prepare a number of clues that will ultimately lead your student leaders from your usual meeting room to either the church sanctuary or an obscure room—where you're hiding. These clues can be easy, difficult, symbolic, or coded; it's your call as long as the students can figure out where to go and eventually find you.

Ask one of your youth leaders to meet your student leaders in your regular meeting place and explain to the team as they arrive that they're going on a search. Before handing out the first clue, have the youth leader read Luke 15:3-7 to your students.

Have your volunteer youth leader say to your team—

Just as God went on an all-out search for his lost sheep, so he is calling us to go on an all-out search for friends and family members that are lost and separated from God. Tonight, you're going out on a search.

At this point, your volunteer youth leader should give out the first clue. As needed, this person can help students figure out the clues that lead to you. When your team finds you in the designated place, ask the students to sit down in a circle and light the candles you've set up around the room. Bring out the guitar and have a time of worship together.

Then discuss these questions—

• **On a scale of 1 to 10, how hard were you searching for the answers to the clues? What determines how hard you look?**

• **What's something you would be willing to give all your effort to search for? Why would you search so hard for it?**

You'll need—
• clues written on slips of paper, prepared ahead of time

• candles

• matches

• worship leader

• guitar or other instrument

Then Jesus told them this parable: "Suppose one of you has a hundred sheep and loses one of them. Does he not leave the ninety-nine in the open country and go after the lost sheep until he finds it? And when he finds it, he joyfully puts it on his shoulders and goes home. Then he calls his friends and neighbors together and says, 'Rejoice with me; I have found my lost sheep.' I tell you that in the same way there will be more rejoicing in heaven over one sinner who repents than over ninety-nine righteous persons who do not need to repent."

—Luke 15:3-7.

• **Compare searching for** [name an item students mentioned for the last question] **and Jesus searching for his lost sheep. What similarities and differences do you notice?**

Remind students that God "looks" hard for each and every lost person so everyone can know him. He uses us in that process, but he doesn't leave us to do the task alone.

Team Huddle *20 min.*

The Soldier and the Boy
Read the following story or tell it in your own words—

From *Hot Illustrations for Youth Talks* by Wayne Rice, Youth Specialties, 1994.

During the War between the States, a young Union soldier lost both his older brother and his father in the battle of Gettysburg. The soldier decided to go to Washington, D.C., to see President Lincoln to ask for an exemption from military services so that he could go back and help his sister and mother with the spring planting on the farm. Having received a furlough from the military to go and plead his case, he arrived in Washington, went to the White House, approached the front gate, and asked to see the president.

"Sorry, young man," replied the guard on duty. "There's a war going on, and the president is very busy." Noticing the soldier's uniform, he added, "You'd best just get back out there on the battle lines where you belong."

Disheartened, the soldier walked to a nearby park bench and sat down, his head in his hands.

"Soldier, you look unhappy. What's wrong?"

The soldier looked up to see a young boy standing in front of him. Something about the child made him spill his heart to him. He told of his father and brother being killed in the war, and of the desperate situation at home. He explained that his mother and sister had no one to help them with the farm.

"I can help you, soldier," the boy said. He took the soldier by the hand and led him back to the front gate of the White House. This time the soldier wasn't stopped...the guard must not have noticed them, the soldier thought. They walked straight to the front door of the White House and walked right in. After they got inside, they walked right past generals and high-ranking officials, and no one said a word. The soldier couldn't understand this. Why didn't anyone try to stop them?

Finally, they reached the Oval Office, which the little boy entered without even knocking on the door. The president was at his desk with the secretary of state, looking over battle plans.

"Good afternoon, Todd," said the president, who then looked at the soldier. "Can you introduce me to your friend?"

"Daddy," said Todd Lincoln, the son of the president, "this soldier needs to talk to you."

Fifteen minutes later the soldier walked out of the White House with his exemption in his pocket.

Help your students analyze the story by asking questions like—

- **How are we like the soldier when we want something from God?**
- **How is the little boy who helps the soldier in need like Jesus?**

Now explain the following to your team—

We have access to God the Father through Jesus, who—the Bible says—intercedes for us. The word *intercede* means approaching God on another person's behalf. That's what Jesus does for us.

The Bible says we can come to him anytime and anywhere. And that includes when we want to reach others for Christ. Jesus wants to reach these people more than we do, and he's already interceding with the Father on their behalf. Of course he will intercede for us as we play our part in reaching them for him.

Three-Step Process for Sharing Your Faith

Distribute copies of **The Plan behind Your Prayers** (pages 155-156), and ask the students to read the **"Prayer Litany"** aloud together.

Now say something like the following to your team—

You'll need—
- copies of **The Plan behind Your Prayers** (pages 155-156)
- Bibles

As we conclude these sessions on peer evangelism, we need to remember this three-step process of sharing our faith.

1. **First, sharing our faith begins with prayer:**

   I urge, then, first of all, that requests, prayers, intercession and thanksgiving be made for everyone…this is good, and pleases God our Savior, who wants all men to be saved and to come to a knowledge of the truth **(1 Timothy 2:1, 3-4)**

   In short, prayer is a powerful spiritual tool.

2. **Sharing our faith continues with care. We need to cultivate those relationships with love. They don't care how much we know until they know how much we care.** (Review ways mentioned in the last session that they can reach their campuses for God.)

3. **We share, share, share.** *(Remind them of the seven evangelism styles: relational, invitation, story, proclamation, initiative, service, intellectual.)*

Praying to Impact Our World for Christ

Your leaders can follow along on the handout as you cover the following points.

Colossians 4:3-4 is the basis for the Open Door Prayer, "And pray for us, too, that God may open a door for our message, so that we may proclaim the mystery of Christ, for which I am in chains. Pray that I may proclaim it clearly, as I should."

Here's a way to pray for our friends that we want to know Jesus.

- *Lord, open the door* for me to speak to _____ about you. Now it may be someone you know well and love dearly or it may be someone you just met on campus. But you can pray, "Lord, I want you to open the door—give me a natural opportunity to speak about you."

- *Lord, open his heart.* When Paul reached the first city on one of his mission trips, he met Lydia, who was a merchant there, at a river. The Bible says (in Acts 16:14-15), "The Lord opened her heart to respond." Why not ask the Lord to open up the heart of the person you're praying for? Ask him to go before you to open his heart.

- *Lord, open my mouth.* This might be the hardest prayer of all. When you ask for this, you'll start noticing opportunities that you might have ignored before—especially for the non-Christians who are on your list. Romans 1:16 says, "I am not ashamed of the gospel, because it is the power of God for the salvation of everyone who believes: first for the Jew, then for the Gentile."

With your group, review the four prayer ideas on the handout: Jesus Prayer, Prayer Triplets, Arrow Prayers, and the 10-Minute All-Night Prayer Meeting. Then, ask your team some of these questions—

- Of all the ideas we've talked about today, what seems most important or exciting to you?

- What prayer suggestion would you like to try?

You'll need—
- copies of **A Concert of Prayer** (page 157)
- Bibles

Team Prayer 25 min.

A Concert of Prayer
Distribute copies of **A Concert of Prayer** (page 157), and divide students into groups of three. Let them pray, following the outline on the handout.

The Plan behind Your Prayers

Prayer litany

But now in Christ Jesus you who once were far away have been brought near through the blood of Christ. For he himself is our peace, who has made the two one and has destroyed the barrier, the dividing wall of hostility. For through him we have access to the Father. Let us then approach the throne of grace with confidence, so that we may receive mercy and find grace to help us in our time of need.

—Ephesians 2:13-14, 18 and Hebrews 4:16

Three-step process for sharing our faith

Prayer

Care

Share, share, share

Praying to impact your world for Christ

The Open Door Prayer

Lord, open the door for me to speak to_____ about you. (Colossians 4:3-4)
Lord, open his heart. (Acts 16:14-15)
Lord, open my mouth. (Romans 1:16-17)

Jesus Prayer

The "Jesus Prayer," significant particularly in the spirituality of Eastern Christianity, is this:
Lord Jesus Christ, Son of God, have mercy on me, a sinner.

An abbreviated version, which may be suitable for your students, is this:
Jesus, I need you… Jesus, I receive you.

As you exhale, say, "Jesus, I need you." Then breathe in, saying, "Jesus, I receive you."

Whatever version of the Jesus Prayer you say, saying it—
  • Reminds you of Christ's presence.
  • Helps you focus on Jesus.
  • Reminds you to live each moment for him.
  • Helps you respond better to tough situations.
  • Can inspire unexpected kindness on your part to those around you.
  • Can prompt you to reach out with God's love to someone who's struggling.

(continued)

Prayer Triplets

A prayer triplet is a group of three youths who—

- Hold one another accountable to pray.
- Pray for the salvation of a total of nine people they know who do not know Jesus.
- Pray for their own personal needs and the spread of the gospel on their campus.

List at least two people who could be a part of your prayer triplet.

List three non-Christians to pray for.

Three areas for prayer are—
- my needs
- my campus
- the world outside my own experience

Arrow Prayers

Offer brief prayers for your friends, teachers, principal, mom, dad, or siblings with arrow prayer—you know, those quick prayers you shoot to the Lord as you come in contact with people throughout the day. Pray for any need you know the person has or for general things that anyone can benefit from, like this: "Lord, help my teacher to experience your love for him in a fresh way today. Amen."

10-Minute All-Night Prayer Meeting

Start at midnight. Teams of teens and a youth leader go to different locations around the city. At each site spend 10 minutes praying for the people who work or live there.

You might go to the local school and pray for friends and teachers. Next, go to friends' homes and pray for them and their families. Then visit the church and pray for the pastor, youth leaders, and the youth ministry or club. Get creative about where you go and what you pray about. Don't forget to spend time praising God at nearby parks, nature preserves, and natural wonders along the way.

A Concert of Prayer

Form groups of three. Take turns praying short and to-the-point prayers, following this format—

Adoration. Praise God for who he is. Focus on his personality. Brag on God. "Lord, you are a great God. You are awesome! I'm amazed when I see your faithful provision for all my needs."

Confession. Have a time of confession, asking God to reveal any thoughts, words, or actions that need to be confessed. Encourage kids to confess their shortcomings openly, but allow a time of silence for confessing sins that students want to keep private. After a period of silence have someone read 1 John 1:9.

Thanksgiving. Give God thanks and celebrate God's blessings, answers to prayer, and gifts.

Silence. Ask God to show you what's on his heart; then take some time to quietly listen to God.

Supplication.

- Allow each person to briefly share a specific need. Pray for those needs.

- Pray for your Five Most Wanted list. You may want to use the Open Door Prayer.

    Lord, open the door for me to speak to _____ about you.
    Lord, open his heart.
    Lord, open my mouth.

- Pray for your church and youth ministry.

- Pray for your youth pastor and youth leaders.

- Pray for the needs of your community, schools, and employers.

- Pray for the president and other government officials.

- Pray for the leadership team members (personal purity, willingness to be obedient, godly lifestyle, devotional life, etc.)

From *Student Leadership Training Manual* by Dennis "Tiger" McLuen & Chuck Wysong. Permission to reproduce this page granted only for use in the buyer's own youth group. www.YouthSpecialties.com

157

Developing Effective Small-Group Leaders

The point
God can use us to lead small groups designed to help each member grow closer to him.

The point, unwrapped
This meeting instructs student leaders how to lead effective small-group discussions.

Where in the Word
Acts, Colossians

Team Building 15 min.

Adopt a Personality Role-Play

Make as many copies of **Adopt a Personality** (page 164) as you need so that each student has a card with a personality on it. Cut the copies into individual cards. If your group is smaller than six, you won't assign every personality card to a student leader. If your group is larger than six, divide students into small groups (with not more than one of each personality in the group). Hand out **Developing Effective Small-Group Leaders** (pages 165-166).

Designate the leader of the discussion as the one—male or female—whose shoe size is closest to 9. Have student leaders work through the Bible study, but group members participate in accordance with the personality on their cards. After five minutes or so, pull the group together to debrief with questions like these—

- **Identify the type of personality each participant was acting out.**

- **Describe the leader's effective methods of handling each personality.**

- **What are some ways to handle the difficulties that arise from each personality?**

- **On a scale of one (easy) to 10 (difficult), how hard is it to manage all the personality types while leading a Bible study? What will make it easier for you?**

Team Huddle 30 min.
Transition by saying something like—

Now let's look at Acts 2:42-47—this time as simply yourself, instead of as the personality you adopted earlier.

You'll need—
- copies of **Adopt a Personality,** cut apart (page 164)
- copies of **Developing Effective Small-Group Leaders** (pages 165-166)

You'll need—
- copies of **Developing Effective Small-Group Leaders** (pages 165-166), from the last activity
- **Small-Group Purpose Statement** transparency (page 167), according to instructions
- overhead projector
- Bibles
- pencils

Session

22

Ask one of your student leaders to read the passage to the entire team. As a group, work through the questions on the handout. When you get to "Why Small Groups?" your leaders can take notes as you present relevant ideas from the following.

Why Small Groups?—Summary of Acts 2:42-47

The early church not only had a large-group gathering in the temple, but they also found it effective to meet in homes—that is, in small groups. To summarize Acts 2:42-47, members of the early church devoted themselves to—

- Instruction (the teaching of God's Word)
- Fellowship (encouraging and loving one another)
- Worship (praying, praising God, and breaking bread)
- Evangelism ("the Lord added to their number daily those who were being saved")

Ask your students—

- **What are the benefits of small groups?** (close friendships, encouragement to grow spiritually, accountability)

- **What is the purpose of small groups?** (Write your own small-group purpose statement on a transparency, or make the Small-Group Purpose Statement on page 167 into a transparency. Place it on the overhead. Review the purpose statement with your students.)

- **What can we do to fulfill our purpose?**

Follow up by saying something like—

The points in our purpose statement may seem like a tall order to fill—and they are, for just one person. But that's where our leadership team comes in. We all have different gifts and skills, and when we use them all together, we can make sure the small groups in our ministry fulfill their purpose. Now let's look at some specific things we can do to be better small-group leaders.

The Role of the Leader

Your student leaders can follow along and take notes on **Developing Effective Small-Group Leaders** as you review each point. You can make the following points and add whatever else is important to you.

- **The leader is a listener.** A good leader gives undivided attention to the speaker through active listening, eye contact, and positive body language. Every person has value in God's eyes and deserves the opportunity to be heard.

- **The leader is prepared.** Discussions are more effective when the leader looks over the lesson and thinks through the answers beforehand. Be sure to understand the main idea of the lesson and have some insights of your own to add.

- **The leader leads people, not meetings.** It's easy to let stimulating information become the focus of your thoughts during preparation. It's important to think about how the lesson's truths and questions might affect each individual.

- **The leader is loyal to the small-group members and the overall youth ministry.** If you don't agree with something that happened at Sunday school, a midweek meeting, or a camp, go directly to the person you have the problem with. Don't let your small group turn into gossip time. Be loyal and committed to the overall youth ministry program.

- **The leader prays for the small-group members.** All our plans to bring life change will be useless without the Holy Spirit's work, both in our preparation and during the meetings. The Bible is full of promises and prayers that can be used on behalf of your individual small-group members. Sometimes you can use these prayers almost word for word as you pray for each individual group member. Substitute their names where it fits, and pray that they would—

  ⊙ *Walk with God.*
  For though I am absent from you in body, I am present with you in spirit and delight to see how orderly you are and how firm your faith in Christ is. So then, just as you received Christ Jesus as Lord, continue to live in him, rooted and built up in him, strengthened in the faith as you were taught, and overflowing with thankfulness.
  —Colossians 2:5-7

  ⊙ *Live the Word.*
  Let the word of Christ dwell in you richly as you teach and admonish one another with all wisdom, and as you sing psalms, hymns and spiritual songs with gratitude in [insert student's names] hearts to God. And whatever you do, whether in word or deed, do it all in the name of the Lord Jesus, giving thanks to God the Father through him.
  —Colossians 3:16-17

  ⊙ *Contribute to the work.*
  We proclaim him, admonishing and teaching everyone with all wisdom, so that we may present everyone perfect in Christ. To this end I labor, struggling with all his energy, which so powerfully works in me.
  —Colossians 1:28-29

  ⊙ *Impact the world.*
  Be wise in the way you act toward outsiders; make the most of every opportunity. Let your conversation be always full of grace, seasoned with salt, so that you may know how to answer everyone.
  —Colossians 4:5-6

Leading an Effective Discussion

Explain to your group—

A good small-group leader helps the members of the group discover truth for themselves—so the leader must develop the ability to ask the right questions. These questions become a springboard for small-group members to discover, understand, and apply biblical truths.

Let's look *at four ways to lead effective discussions.*

At this point ask your teams to move back into the groups they were in at the beginning of the session. (Let the leader of each group be the one whose birthday is closest to December 25.)

You'll need—
- copies of **Launching Questions for Small Groups** (page 168)

Session

22

Say to your team something like—
1. *Launching a discussion.*

The first step in leading an effective discussion is launching it. Launching questions are nonthreatening, and anyone can answer them.

Distribute copies of **Launching Questions for Small Groups** (page 168). These questions break the ice and get the group talking and listening. There are 50 or so listed on the handout.

Now you might say—

One of you in each group practice launching a discussion by selecting a question from the list, and offering to go first in answering it. Remember, the more candid you are in your response to the question, the more candid others' answers will be, too. The leader sets the tone.

Have teams discuss this issue for a few minutes. Then move on to the following—

2. *Guiding a discussion.*

The second step in leading an effective small-group discussion is guiding the discussion. Keep the discussion moving, and draw out the main idea that your group is exploring. You can ask questions like—

- **Anyone else want to comment on that?**
- **What does someone else see in the verse?**
- **What exactly do you mean by that?**

Now and then a group gets off track. When that happens, you may need to say something like, "Interesting stuff! Yet we're straying some from the main point...let's finish it first, then come back and tackle this if we want." Then move them right back to the issue at hand.

Avoid asking yes-or-no questions, like "Do you agree with this?" Instead ask open-ended questions like—

- **What do you think about—?**
- **Why do you think so?**

Why, what, and how questions are typically good open-ended questions. Let's practice guiding a discussion by answering the following questions in your small groups.

Have groups choose the person with a birthday closest to July 4 to be leader—then say something like—

Leaders, ask your group a why, what, or how question based somehow on Acts 2:42-47.

If leaders are at a loss, you can always kick this question to the group: *According to Acts 2:42-47, why should small groups be important to our ministry?*
    After they finish, say to your team—

3. *Summarizing a discussion.*

The third step in leading an effective small-group discussion: summarize the discussion—that is, piece it together and describe in a sentence or two where the discussion has gone so far. You'll probably want to do this frequently throughout the group's time together to keep the discussion on track.

Summarizing can also be a transition into the next part of the discussion. But first let's practice summarizing: let's hear someone from each group— *not* the leader—summarize in a couple sentences what your group explored in your *why*, *what*, or *how* question.

When they're done, say to your team—

4. *Helping group members apply what they've learned.*

The fourth step in leading an effective small-group discussion: help group members apply what they've learned. In fact, this is pretty much the definition of discipleship—helping people connect their beliefs to their behavior.

Ask your team a closing question like one of these—

- **How would you like to apply one of the truths we've just covered to your ministry or your life?**

- **What specific role are you willing to play as we seek to have vital small groups within our youth ministry?**

Team Prayer *5 min.*

Close your time in prayer by asking God—

- To help your youth ministry students build closer relationships with Jesus and each other.
- To develop community and friendship in the small group.
- To help students process and act on what they learn from the Bible.
- To change every student for the better who comes into contact with your youth ministry.

Adopt a Personality
The Talker
- never stops talking
- has a comment for everything

Adopt a Personality
The Peacemaker
- can't stand conflict or disagreements
- tries to help everyone get along

Adopt a Personality
The Church Kid
- grew up in church
- has all the right answers
- says "just pray about it" a lot

Adopt a Personality
The Clown
- distracts everyone in the group with sarcastic humor
- can't sit still

Adopt a Personality
The Crisis Mode Kid
- always in a crisis
- gives a personal illustration for everything

Adopt a Personality
The Silent One
- sits and listens
- only contributes if asked

Developing Effective Small-Group Leaders

The Early Church: Acts 2:42-47

What does it say?
[observation]

1. On what four areas did the new believers focus? (2:42)

2. How did the new believers approach these four areas? (2:42)

3. What unusual deeds did the apostles do? (2:43)

4. How did the people respond? (2:43)

5. What lifestyle did the early believers adopt? (2:44-45)

6. How did the early believers meet together? (2:46-47)

7. What were the results? (2:47)

What does it mean?
[interpretation]

1. Why is it important that members of the early church met in the temple courts and in their homes?

2. Why were small groups so important to the growth and health of the early church?

3. What does that say about the need for small groups in our youth ministry?

4. How do the activities of the early church compare to the activities of our church?

What should I do?
[application]

1. How could our youth ministry be more like the early church?

(continued)

2. What effect do you think these changes could have on our youth ministry?

3. What can you do to help our youth ministry become more like the early church?

4. Have you ever been in a small group that really made a difference in your Christian life? If so, what difference did it make?

5. What purpose should small groups serve in our ministry?

6. What role would you like to play in small groups within our ministry?

Why Small Groups? *[summary of Acts 2:42-47]*

• Instruction

• Fellowship

• Worship

• Evangelism

The Role of the Leader

The leader—
• Is a listener

• Is prepared

• Leads people, not meetings

• Is committed to the small-group members and the overall youth ministry

• Prays for the small-group members

Leading an Effective Discussion

The leader—
• Launches the discussion

• Guides the discussion

• Summarizes the discussion

• Helps group members apply what they have learned

The purpose of our small groups is to provide a caring atmosphere where we can—

- Build closer relationships with Jesus through God's Word, prayer, and conversation with each other.

- Provide community and friendship for each other.

- Help each other process and act on what we learn from God.

- Promote life change by allowing people to ask candid, honest questions.

Launching Questions for Small Groups

Describe a memorable birthday celebration.

Name your favorite magazine and explain the reason why it's your favorite.

Where were you living between the ages of seven and 11? What was it like?

If money were no object, describe your ideal, week-long vacation.

If you could see any musical group perform live, who would it be? Why?

If you could spend the day with any celebrity, who would it be? What would you do together?

If you were diagnosed with cancer, what would be your one wish before you died?

What is your most cherished possession and why?

Who has been the most influential person in your life and why?

Describe your favorite room in your house and why.

What was your favorite movie of all time? Why did you like it?

Describe your favorite memory with a pet of yours (a pet that belonged to someone else).

What do you want your tombstone to say and why?

What one skill do you wish you could learn? Explain why.

Describe your worst experience in a church.

Describe your best experience in a church.

What offends you and why?

Summarize in one sentence a message your dad or mom clearly communicated to you while you were growing up.

What has been your favorite summer vacation?

Share the story of how you got one of your scars.

What would be the worst kind of insult a person could give you?

When was the last time you cried? What was the cause?

What do you consider your greatest accomplishment?

What was the worst decision you made this year?

What do you consider to be your worst failure this year?

Describe your most embarrassing moment.

When have you had your heart broken? What happened?

What is your favorite holiday and why?

If you could have any job, what would it be and why?

If you could visit anywhere in the world, where would it be and why?

Finish this sentence: I feel rebellious when...

Describe the last time you got physically hurt.

What is one food you love and one you can't stand?

What's the biggest problem on your campus?

Finish this sentence: If I could change one thing about my school I would...

Describe your family on Mondays at 6 p.m. Who's home and what's everyone doing?

Do you think guys or girls have it tougher in junior high school?

What's your typical response to a mistake?

When does your family do chores? What are your regular responsibilities?

Share about a time when you lied and got into big trouble.

Who do you think matures faster—girls or guys? In what ways?

If you could change one thing about your family, what would it be?

What are the three most important rules in your family?

Describe a time when you were grounded, but it was totally unfair.

Describe the last time you lost your temper.

What is the toughest part of growing up?

What is the nicest compliment a person could give you?

Describe a time when you took a huge risk. How did it turn out?

What's one thing you wish Jesus had never said?

If someone were to say to you, "You're just like your mom [or dad]," what might they mean?

If you had to pick an age to be for the rest of your life, what would it be and why?

ministry teams

Who Gets the Glory?

The point

Whatever you do, do it for God's glory.

The point, unwrapped

Typically, one of a student leader's duties is to plan and implement programs—which includes being up front and visible during programs. This session helps students understand that when they are up front, they must make it their goal to draw attention to Christ, not to themselves.

Where in the Word

1 Corinthians, Philippians

Team Building *15 min.*

Before your team arrives, inconspicuously set up a video camera to record the meeting. A few minutes before you expect students to arrive, press the record button.

All Scrambled Up

Using one word of 1 Corinthians 10:31 per card, prepare one set of index cards for every group of four to six students. Give each group its set of cards. At the signal, the groups compete to unscramble the passage the fastest.

Bumper Stickers

While still in the groups from the last activity, pass out the paper and pens and direct students to create a bumper sticker slogan that sums up the meaning of 1 Corinthians 10:31. Let the teams share their bumper stickers.

Now ask your student leaders—

- **What observations can we make about God from this verse? About us?**

- **How can we apply this verse to what our student leadership team does?**

Now say something like—

Leadership is a funny thing. In one sense, yes, you're the ones leading games, giving your testimonies, leading worship, maybe even giving talks. Yet at the same time, you must also be the ones to constantly remind yourself of who gets the glory. "Whatever we do," someone said, "we do it as to an audience of two"—which means, among other things, that we should live our lives thinking not what others think of us, but ultimately what *you* and *God* think.

So what is it like to know that God watches all we do and are? This may be just a taste of it...

Remove the tape from the camera, cue it to the beginning of the first game and prepare for belly laughs as you watch yourselves on tape.

You'll need—

- video camera
- video tape
- index cards, each with one of the following words written on it (write the reference on one card): SO WHETHER YOU EAT OR DRINK OR WHATEVER YOU DO, DO IT ALL FOR THE GLORY OF GOD. 1 CORINTHIANS 10:31, one set for each group.
- sheets of paper, one per group
- pencil or pen for each group
- VCR
- TV

Team Huddle *10 min.*

Discuss some of these questions—

- **What's your reaction to seeing yourself recorded on a hidden camera?**

- **If you had known ahead of time that you were being videotaped, would you have done anything differently? If so, what and why?**

- **Think about doing everything for God's glory. What would you do differently?**

- **How does the idea of doing everything for God's glory apply to serving as a student leader in our youth ministry?**

You'll need—

- copies of **Who Gets the Glory?** (page 171)

- Bibles

- pencils

Team Study *20 min.*

Begin the next activity by saying something along these lines—

In this session we're going to focus on who gets the glory in our ministries—do we or does God? Take out your Bibles and open them to Philippians 2:1-11.

Ask one of your student leaders to read the passage to the entire team. Pass out **Who Gets the Glory?** (page 171) and pencils. Have your kids complete and discuss this handout in small groups. When they've finished, you might say to your team—

When we're up front [mention activities your teens might be performing—leading songs, leading games, sharing testimonies, giving talks, greeting students, setting up chairs], **we need to have a different attitude. First, we're in God's presence. Second, every person who walks through the door matters to God. Our number one goal is to serve Christ first and then point others to him, not to ourselves.**

Team Prayer *5 min.*

Close this session by asking your student leadership team to reflect in silence as you read a letter from God—

Dear friends,

I have created you. I've called you by name. You are precious in my sight, and I rejoice over you with joy. In fact, I called you into fellowship with my son, Jesus. I taught you how to walk in my ways, though you may not have realized it. So seek me day by day, and delight to know my ways.

Press on to know me, and I will respond to you as surely as the coming of the dawn or the rain of early spring. Come and behold my beauty. Pour out your heart to me like water, and know the refreshment that comes from my presence. So whether you eat or drink or whatever you do, do it all for my glory and I will lift you up and bless you.

Love always,

Your heavenly Father

From *Memory Makers*, by Doug Fields and Duffy Robbins (Zondervan, 1996).

Who Gets the Glory?
Philippians 2:1-11

What does it say?
[observation]

1. What four qualities mark unity with Christ? (2:1)

2. How can Christians show their unity in Christ in practical ways? (2:2)

3. What did Paul say about self-centeredness? (2:3-4)

4. What did Paul encourage followers of Christ to have? (2:5)

5. What did Jesus set aside when he became a man? (2:6-8)

6. What was the ultimate result of Jesus humbling himself and dying on the cross? (2:9-11)

What does it mean?
[interpretation]

1. What attitudes should we reflect as leaders?

What should I do?
[application]

1. What grade (A-F) would you give our up-front leadership in the area of pointing to Christ and not to ourselves? Why? (If not an A, what do we need to do to get an A?)

2. What things might we do as leaders that potentially draw attention to us and away from God? What does it take to point people to God instead?

3. If the purpose of our ministry is to point people to God, how can we do that?

4. What can we do as a ministry team to be more like Jesus in Philippians 2?

5. What practical steps can you take this week to demonstrate an attitude of humility in your specific area of ministry?

Leading with Excellence

The point
God deserves your best.

The point, unwrapped
The effort we exert in practicing and training is an important ingredient to our ministry.

Where in the Word
1 Corinthians, Colossians, 2 Timothy

Team Building *10 min.*
Divide students into groups of three or four and distribute pencils and copies of **Practice Makes Perfect** (pages 175-176) to each student. Have the groups answer the first four questions, then come back together to compile a master list of activities from Question 3 on a whiteboard. Comment on the wide variety of activities that require practice.
   Then say something like—

Our lives are filled with things that require hard work and practice. However, when it comes to our spiritual lives, and sometimes our ministries, we relax a little. We want to trust God's grace and not do the hard work behind the scenes. We're going to study the value of practicing today.

Team Huddle *5 min.*
Have the students complete the "Spiritual Discipline Self-Assessment" section of the handout.
   Then say something like—

Discipline is often the hard work behind the scenes. It's one thing to pray during a church service or youth ministry meeting, but it's a completely different thing to have the discipline to pray every morning before you go to school. Serving on a ministry team requires practice and discipline behind the scenes as well. Today we want to look at this issue of leading with excellence for the sake of our ministry.

Team Study *30 min.*
In groups have the students read the Bible passages and respond to the questions on **Practice Makes Perfect**. Bring your teens back together for a large group discussion when they're finished.

You'll need—
- copies of **Practice Makes Perfect** (pages 175-176)
- pencils
- whiteboard and markers

You'll need—
- copies of **Practice Makes Perfect** (pages 175-176), from the previous activity
- pencils

You'll need—
- copies of **Practice Makes Perfect** (pages 175-176) from the last activity
- Bibles
- pencils

Conclude by asking a student to summarize the main ideas of the discussion (hopefully it's along the lines of this: we work hard and practice to honor God and be more effective in ministry. God deserves our best, so it's important to strive for excellence. Practice is part of our service).

Team Prayer *5 min.*

End your session in conversational prayer. You might have each leader thank God for an idea he learned during the session or for wisdom and strength to do what he knows he should. Students can ask for good attitudes and willingness to go the extra mile.

Practice Makes Perfect

What do you do well?

- Okay, time to show off: do a bizarre trick or talent you have. You know, demonstrate your double-jointedness, fold your tongue lengthwise, balance a pencil on your nose. Whatever.

- If you could cultivate any talent, what would it be? Why?

- Write here the things you do that required practice—like drama or choir rehearsal, team practice, etc.

Spiritual discipline self-assessment

Rate yourself in the following areas.

Praying

I've never been better at this	I'm doing pretty good at this	I'm better some days than others	I need help with this, and fast

Reading the Bible

I've never been better at this	I'm doing pretty good at this	I'm better some days than others	I need help with this, and fast

Attending worship regularly

I've never been better at this	I'm doing pretty good at this	I'm better some days than others	I need help with this, and fast

Giving

I've never been better at this	I'm doing pretty good at this	I'm better some days than others	I need help with this, and fast

Loving my family

I've never been better at this	I'm doing pretty good at this	I'm better some days than others	I need help with this, and fast

Sharing my faith with others

I've never been better at this	I'm doing pretty good at this	I'm better some days than others	I need help with this, and fast

Attending leadership meetings

I've never been better at this	I'm doing pretty good at this	I'm better some days than others	I need help with this, and fast

Finishing homework & attending school

I've never been better at this	I'm doing pretty good at this	I'm better some days than others	I need help with this, and fast

(continued)

Open the Bible!

Colossians 3:17; 4:2-6

1. According to Colossians 3:17, what's the focus of our ministry?

2. List the commands Paul gives in Chapter 4 verses you read.

3. What do these verses have to do with pursuing excellence?

4. Of the several ideas that may have come to mind about how you could change or redirect your life, write down one of them here. How can you do it?

1 Corinthians 9:24-25

5. Think about our list of activities that require practice. If the apostle Paul (the writer of these verses) were sitting among you, what do you think he'd say about those activities?

6. What kind of practive and training do you need to pursue as a leader in our youth ministry?

7. What's one specific way you can pursue that practice and training this week?

2 Timothy 2:1-7

8. What' are the three different word pictures used in this passage? What role do discipline and practice have in each of them?

9. Which one of Paul's analogies, or word pictures, inspires you the most? Or what analogy would fit you better?

10. What will that word picture inspire you to do this week?

The Call to Christ Is the Call to Serve—Motivation

The point
Leading by serving.

The point, unwrapped
Here student leaders explore their motivation for serving others. They look at the example of Jesus' life—especially how, although he was the son of God, he chose to serve others rather than insist on being served by them. Your kids will compare two leadership models: the model of the world, and the model of Jesus *(which is really a servant-leader model)*.

Where in the Word
Mark, Philippians

Team Building *10 min.*

Coin Give-a-Way
Begin by distributing the coins, three or four to each person. It's not important that everyone begins with the same number of coins.

During the first round the objective is for students to get as many coins as possible. They may ask for a coin from any other player, who must give one when asked. You may want to add a rule about only asking for one coin and then moving to another player. Of course, they *all* are available to be asked for coins, and they can't take coins by force. Play for one minute.

Play a second round but this time reverse it. Students give away as many coins as possible in one minute.

When you're finished, debrief with these questions or other you think of—

You'll need—
- enough coins so every member of the leadership team can have three or four

- **What strategies did you use to try to get coins? To give coins?**

- **How did you feel when coins were given to you? When coins were taken from you?** (If the feelings were different, ask why they weren't the same for both rounds.)

- **Giving and receiving coins is a little like giving acts of service to others and receiving acts of service from others. Explain how.**

- **Explain what we can learn about serving based on the game.**

Jesus came as a servant. We're called to be like Jesus, so we are to be servants, too.

Session 26

Team Huddle *15 min.*

Pass out 20 slips of paper and ask students to collectively write down 20 different famous people—one on each slip. They can be living or dead, from all walks of life. Collect the papers and put them into a box at the front of the room. Lay the string on the floor. It's a continuum with one end representing people who are humble, caring servants and the other representing those who are egotistical and selfish.

Have each member of the leadership team (one at a time) draw one of the names and place the paper on the string according to how they view the famous person's servant attitude. Keep going until all the names have been drawn.

Discuss as a group how they decided where to place the names they drew. Ask them questions like these—

- **Which of these people would you consider to be great leaders? Which do you think were also servants? Explain your thinking.**

- **What would God think about these people as leaders and as servants?**

- **How does being a servant help a person be a great leader?**

Then say—

I have one more name I'd like to place on the string.

Hand someone a slip with *JESUS CHRIST* written on it and have him place it on the continuum. Then say something like—

Obviously Jesus was a great leader, yet he also served other people. Today we are going to take a look at Jesus and his attitude toward service. We'll see from his example how being a servant makes someone a great leader. Then we'll evaluate our own attitude toward service in light of Jesus' commands and example.

Team Study *20 min.*

Have your leadership team get into groups of four or five (or smaller if you have a small leadership team) and take about eight minutes to complete the first section of **The Call to Christ Is the Call to Serve—Motivation** (page 180). Assign each team one of the passages and have them give a brief report to the rest of the group about their answers.

Talkback

After the students have finished reporting to the rest of the group, you might say—

If we read the verses following those we just looked at in Philippians, we see that, although Jesus was God, he didn't hold on to his rights and privileges as God. He gave them all up and came to earth as a man. While he

was on earth he humbled himself and became obedient—all the way to a terrible death on the cross.

It had to be difficult for Jesus to do this, yet he did. God, through Paul, asks us to have the same attitude Jesus had. I'd like you to consider a few questions as we close this session and pray together.

Go over "**Self-Assessment**" on the handout with the students.

Team Prayer *20 min.*

End this session by praying as a team conversationally. Your teens can pray that each student leader would, in the coming week, be aware of opportunities to give up their rights and take action by serving others. They can also ask God for help to become the leaders the Lord wants them to be.

The Call to Christ
Is the Call to Serve—Motivation

Read the passage assigned to your group and answer the questions together. Choose a spokesperson to report back to the entire group.

Mark 10:42-45

1. According to Jesus, what is the key to being great in the kingdom of God? Why did God go with this way of establishing greatness?

2. Explain what *slave of all* means.

3. Name some ways Jesus showed that he was a servant.

Philippians 2:1-8

1. According to these verses, what should our attitude be toward other people? Now put that idea into your own words.

2. What does this passage say about our own interests?

3. Do you think it's possible for someone to look not only to her own interests, but also to the interests of others? Why or why not?

Self-Assessment

1. Rate your attitude as a servant on a scale of one to 10, with one being a selfish pig and 10 being a Jesus clone. Explain why you gave yourself that rating.

2. Where would you like to rate instead? Why?

3. Write down two practical ways you will serve someone this week, in the youth group, at school, at work, at home. Be specific.

The Call to Christ Is the Call to Serve— Servanthood

The point
Student leaders will brainstorm practical ways to serve others.

The point, unwrapped
By looking, really *looking*, at the needs of people around them—people they rub shoulders with every day—they can deliberately plan to help meet some of those needs, whether individually or as a group.

Where in the Word
John

Team Building *10 min.*

Personal Piles
If your group is larger than 6 or 8 students, divide into groups of 4 or so. Ask students to dig through their wallets, purses, or backpacks and take out several items each that are valuable to them, or that represent something valuable to them—then put them in a common pile in the middle of the group. Now everyone in the group gets to go through the pile, checking out what the others value, asking questions, telling whatever stories inevitably lie behind some of the items.

Make sure all the personal items get back to the rightful owners, then ask questions like these—

- **What besides money was in your group's Personal Pile?**

- **Any photos? Of whom?**

- **What new thing did you learn about a person in your group?**

- **Why do you keep some of those items with you?**

It's probably easy to keep such items in your wallet or purse—they mean a lot to you. It may just look like an old ticket stub or a crumpled note or a Chinese fortune cookie—but that simple object probably recreates or at least reminds you of people, places, happenings, or emotions associated with that object. There's a lot of natural motivation in things we have strong emotional connections with.

But what about things we ought to feel strongly about, but don't—naturally, at least? Particularly this: everyone knows that God expects us to "love one another." But what does that mean? Who exactly is "one another"? What if the "one anothers" mean zilch to you?

In this session we'll explore how we can show God's love to people whose pictures haven't made it into our wallets.

Session

26

Team Huddle *15 min.*

Designate one wall of the room for people who agree with the statement you will read, and designate the opposite wall for people who disagree.

To be moved by the needs of those around us means nothing, unless we do *something* to meet those needs. To be touched by the pain of hurting people is useless, unless we somehow touch those who are hurting.

Repeat it once or twice to make sure they understand before they move. Let the two groups discuss their positions and defend them.

Ask—

Why do you think there is so much difference between the way we feel about the needs of those around us and what we do in response to them?

Have your students form groups of three and brainstorm to come up with the five greatest needs of the people around them. Examples could be loneliness, lack of financial resources, lack of self-esteem, and so on. Be sure to pass out paper and pencils. Come back together as a large group and try to agree on the top 10 needs. List them on a whiteboard.

Ask—

- **Is it our responsibility as Christians to try to meet the needs of the people around us? Why or why not?**

- **What does it take to motivate us to action when we see others in need?**

Team Study *15 min.*

Now you could say—

As Christians we have been called to meet the needs of those around us. But unless we take time to get to know the people we go to school with, work with, and live around, we will never know their needs. Even after getting to know someone, we may not understand their needs unless we're consciously alert for them. In the story we are about to read, Jesus saw a need and met it.

Move into groups of three or four and pass out **The Call to Christ Is the Call to Serve— Servanthood** (page 184). Each group should take five minutes to read the Scripture passages and answer the questions that follow. Meet back together to share insights.

Talkback

Then say something like—

As leaders, if we're going to follow Jesus' example and meet the needs of the people around us, we first have to take the time to understand their

You'll need—

- whiteboard and markers
- paper
- pencils

You'll need—

- copies of **The Call to Christ Is the Call to Serve—Servanthood** (page 184)
- Bibles
- pencils
- copies of **The Call to Christ Is the Call to Serve Business Cards** (page 185), made on card stock if possible

needs. We have to learn about their hurts and struggles if we're going to be able to do anything to help. But once we have discovered the needs, we have to decide that we're going to step out and do something. It's too easy to get stuck between the point of awareness and caring and the point of doing. I'd like to close our time together today by giving each of you something to add to your wallets.

Give your student leaders a printed business card cut from **The Call to Christ Is the Call to Serve Business Cards** sheet (page 185). Read one aloud as students place them in their wallets. Then ask—

What is one specific way you'll put into practice what you learned today?

Team Prayer *20 min.*

End your session in prayer. Some ideas:

• Ask God to open the eyes of the leadership team members to see the needs of those around them.
• Ask him to help them be compassionate toward those in need.
• Ask God for direction about needs he's calling students to help meet.

The Call to Christ is the Call to Serve—Servanthood

Read the passage assigned to your group and answer the questions.

John 13:1-5, 12-17

1. Try to put yourself in Jesus' shoes at the time this took place. What kind of pressure was he under?

2. If you were facing something as horrible as the crucifixion, would you have been concerned about the needs of other people? Why or why not?

3. Why do you think Jesus, facing the most stressful time of his life, stopped to wash the disciples' feet?

4. After Jesus encouraged the disciples to follow his example, he told them, "Now that you know these things, you will be blessed if you do them." How wide is the gap between what you know you should do and what you actually do? Explain your answer. What can you do to bridge the gap?

5. What are some of the needs around you—perhaps needs of other students on the team—that Jesus might like you to meet? What can you do about one of them?

The call to Christ is the call to serve.

You need to **know...**
    You need to **care...**
        You need to **do.**

I can do everything through him who gives me strength.
    –Philippians 4:13

You have never looked into the eyes of another person who isn't important to God–and everyone who matters to God should matter to me.

The call to Christ is the call to serve.

You need to **know...**
    You need to **care...**
        You need to **do.**

I can do everything through him who gives me strength.
    –Philippians 4:13

You have never looked into the eyes of another person who isn't important to God–and everyone who matters to God should matter to me.

The call to Christ is the call to serve.

You need to **know...**
    You need to **care...**
        You need to **do.**

I can do everything through him who gives me strength.
    –Philippians 4:13

You have never looked into the eyes of another person who isn't important to God–and everyone who matters to God should matter to me.

The call to Christ is the call to serve.

You need to **know...**
    You need to **care...**
        You need to **do.**

I can do everything through him who gives me strength.
    –Philippians 4:13

You have never looked into the eyes of another person who isn't important to God–and everyone who matters to God should matter to me.

The call to Christ is the call to serve.

You need to **know...**
    You need to **care...**
        You need to **do.**

I can do everything through him who gives me strength.
    –Philippians 4:13

You have never looked into the eyes of another person who isn't important to God–and everyone who matters to God should matter to me.

The call to Christ is the call to serve.

You need to **know...**
    You need to **care...**
        You need to **do.**

I can do everything through him who gives me strength.
    –Philippians 4:13

You have never looked into the eyes of another person who isn't important to God–and everyone who matters to God should matter to me.

The Leadership Program—The Plan

The point
Developing a strategy for your youth ministry.

The point, unwrapped
This meeting leads students in exploring the big picture of purposeful programming.

Where in the Word
Matthew

Team Building *10 min.*

Keeping the Goal in Sight
When planning and developing a program or event, it's easy to lose sight of the goal for it. Read **Keeping the Goal in Sight** or tell it in your own words.

Keeping the Goal in Sight

The California coast was shrouded in fog that Fourth of July morning in 1952. Twenty-one miles to the west, on Catalina Island, a 34-year-old woman waded into the water and began swimming toward California, determined to be the first woman to do so. Her name was Florence Chadwick, and she had already been the first woman to swim the English Channel in both directions.

The water was numbing cold that July morning, and the fog was so thick she could hardly see the boats in her own party. Millions were watching on national television. Several times sharks, which had gotten too close, had to be driven away with rifles to protect the lone figure in the water. As the hours ticked off, she swam on. Fatigue had never been her big problem in these swims—it was the bone-chilling cold of the water.

After more than 15 hours, numbed with the cold, she asked to be taken out. She couldn't go on. Her mother and her trainer, alongside in a boat, told her they were near land. They urged her not to quit. But when she looked toward the California coast, all she could see was the dense fog.

After 15 hours and 55 minutes she was taken out of the water. It was not until hours later, when her body began to thaw, that she felt the shock of failure. To a reporter she blurted out, "Look, I'm not excusing myself. But if I could have seen land, I might have made it."

She had been pulled out only half a mile from the California coast! Later she was to reflect that she had been beaten not by fatigue or even the cold—the fog alone defeated her because it obscured her goal. It had blinded her eyes, her heart, and her desire.

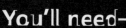
It was the only time Florence Chadwick ever quit. Two months later she swam that same channel, and again the fog obscured her view, but this time she swam with her faith intact. Somewhere behind that fog was land. Not only was she the first woman to swim the Catalina Channel, but she beat the men's record by two hours!

Ask your students—

- **Why were the outcomes of the first and second swims different?**

- **When do you feel like giving up on a dream or goal?**

- **What keeps you going when pursuing a goal gets tough?**

- **"Plans fail for lack of counsel," says Proverbs 15:22, "but with many advisers they succeed." What in your own life could you use the advice of a counselor for?**

Team Huddle *30 min.*

Begin by saying something like the following to your team—

Today let's focus on our youth ministry's big picture. Why do we do what we do? Why do we have outreach nights and Bible studies and mission trips? You know our goal isn't to keep everyone busy because we don't have anything better to do. But do you know what the purposes *are*? After today, we'll know our purposes and goals. And *that* will help when things get difficult.

Hand out the copies of **Reaching Friends Where They Are** (page 190)—or show the transparency on the overhead projector). Now you might say to your team—

In developing effective plans for our youth ministry, we need a clear picture of where our friends are at spiritually so we know how to impact them. Almost every student on your campus is going to fall into one of four categories. It's important to remember before we do this that this isn't some ladder of spirituality. What we're trying to do is to identify where our friends are at so we know how to reach them effectively.

Talk through the sheet with your team. Now give students a few minutes to write down the names or initials of friends, relatives, and neighbors under the category that represents their current level of spiritual interest. (Don't write down anyone on the leadership team.)
Then ask your team—

- **Which category did most of your friends fall into?**

- **Why is it important to have an idea where your friends are at spiritually?**

- **Why is this exercise important for our youth ministry?**

Have a student read Matthew 28:18-20. Continue by saying something like—

You'll need—

- overhead projector

- copies of **Reaching Friends Where They Are** (page 190) for each student, or a transparency made from that page

- paper

- pencils

- copies of **So What's the Game Plan** (pages 191-193)

- Bibles

- copies of **Program Planning Worksheet** (page 194)

This Bible passage is not called the Great Suggestion, but the Great Commission. Jesus doesn't tell us to go and make casual believers or curious people, but to go and make *disciples* of all nations. The goal is to see people transformed into devoted followers of Christ.

Since Jesus gives us this command, it should be at least one of our youth ministry goals. How is our youth ministry going to reach our friends and help them come to know, love, and follow Jesus Christ wholeheartedly? *[Give students an opportunity to respond.]*

The challenge is to keep *outreach, growth,* and *ministry* in balance. We have friends that fall into each of those three categories. It only makes sense that to reach all of our friends, we need to have a plan that provides opportunities in each of those three areas.

Have your student leaders begin brainstorming ideas for—

• **Outreach** (including welcoming and affirming guests and visitors)
• **Growth** (including small-group ministry, Bible studies, and personal devotional life)
• **Service** (whether in your church, around your community, out of state, or international)

Students can list events, camps, programs, or Bible studies that they've experienced or that are new. A few ideas for each category are provided to get you going (see **So What's the Game Plan?** on pages 191-193), but pull out your *Ideas Library* or other youth ministry resources and let your students begin planning for a balanced youth ministry.

When your team is ready to plug some of these ideas (or their own ideas) into a specific program, you can use the **Program Planning Worksheet** (page 194) to lay out the details of your program.

Team Prayer *10 min.*
Close by asking God to guide you in your plans for the year.

Reaching Friends Where They Are

Crowd—*not ready to visit*

These students represent the teenage population in your general geographical sphere of influence. You may not have influence on these students right now, but you know about them. These people—
- Have little or no knowledge of God.
- Do not attend church unless obligated to go to a funeral or wedding.
- Do not listen to religious radio or TV programs except by accident, in which case they only listen long enough to recharge their defenses.
- Were the main audience Jesus took his message to.

Crowd friends, relatives, neighbors:

Casual—*ready to visit*

These students may be visiting for the first time or may be attending regularly. They may be churched or unchurched. They may be there because your outreach ministry attracted them or just because they will follow you anywhere. These people—
- Are community students who are just visiting youth group or church, or are churched students who don't take their faith seriously.
- Are attending your youth group's fun events, but little else.
- Wouldn't claim a relationship with Christ.
- Are unaware of or don't care about spiritual things.

Casual friends, relatives, neighbors:

Curious—*ready to grow*

These students have started a relationship with Christ and are interested in growing spiritually. These people—
- Are beginning to take their faith seriously.
- Are attending youth group or church consistently.
- Demonstrate a desire to grow through words and actions.
- Ask questions about their faith.

Curious friends, relatives, neighbors:

Committed—*ready to serve*

These students want to make a difference with their lives. These people—
- Have a heart to be obedient to God.
- Are attentive and open.
- Are beginning to understand the implications of their faith.
- Are willing to serve.
- Are attempting to influence their friends.

Committed friends, relatives, neighbors:

So What's the Game Plan?

crowd & casual students
Ideas for outreach—*including welcoming and affirming guests and visitors*

Youth Group Hotline
You'll need a dedicated phone line, an answering machine, and business cards.
- Set up a youth group phone line with its own number. The phone company can arrange one for you at reasonable rates. The phone company might also help you find a number that's easy for kids to remember (385-YOUTH, or 29-THE SON, or GET-READY, or THE-STING, or whatever).
- If you can't get the number you want, at least give the hotline a clever name.
- Hook up a telephone answering machine.
- Now record the annoucement. Of course, you can make it anything you want—the current week's activities and meetings, a monthly calendar, a devotional, a reminder that this Sunday is the deadline to get their deposits to you for camp.

  But to customize this idea for outreach purposes, record an annoucement that is tailored to unchurched callers. That means no religious jargon or evangelistic hype, but rather be appealing, inviting, helpful, and informative. Consider having a student record the announcement, which can tell callers about the exciting stuff your youth group is doing, where and when your group meets, a number to call if a caller needs help or counseling, maybe a bit of entertaining fluff ("Finally, a reminder that this is Kayak Safety Week—so keep those paddles from flailing into other kayakers' personal space, okay?").
- At whatever copy shop is nearby, print up some business cards with the phone number and some compelling text that will tease unchurched kids into calling the number. Youth group students can distribute these to friends on their campuses.

Campus Newspaper Ads
Place an ad for your youth group in your high schools' newspapers. The ad can be a—
- Testimony of one of your youth group members, preferably a student in that school.
- Promotion of an upcoming event that is particularly appropriate to unchurched kids—party, retreat, outreach event, etc.
- Congratulation to a campus group or team (rather than to an individual) for a championship, performance, achievement, etc.
- ...or anything that serves your youth group's purpose of outreach.
  And always identify your youth group by name and numbers (phone, location, Web site, etc.).

Class Wars
Take four weeks and have Class War competitions between the freshmen, sophomores, juniors, and seniors. Give out points for the class with the highest attendance, participation points, game points, etc. The class that wins is rewarded with a free pizza bash or the youth pastor's Mercedes, etc. (If your group is small, try combining the freshmen with the seniors and the sophomores with the juniors.)

Student Scavenger Hunt
This scavenger hunt is designed to dramatically increase the attendance of your youth ministry in one evening. Divide into groups of four. Each group has a car and a driver. You have 45 minutes to find and bring back to the youth group as many high school students as possible.

   Tell your friends it will only be a half an hour. The winning team gets a prize to be announced. Create a long list with points for each.

(continued)

Ideas for the scavenger hunt are—
- Ninth grade boy—100 points
- Ninth grade girl—100 points
- Sophomore girl with braces—300 points
- Sophomore boy with braces—300 points
- Senior class president—300 points
- A couple who are dating each other—500 points
- A junior who has never been to the group before—500 points
- A teacher or a counselor—1000 points
- A principal—2000 points
- A student that can juggle—400 points
- A student wearing pajamas—500 points
- A student who brings a gift to the youth leader—700 points

Add as many categories as you want. When the students come back, provide lots of food, have some music blasting, let one of the student leaders share a testimony, and then give a brief (three to four minutes) wrap-up with information about your next meeting or camp.

Door Knob Encouragement
A fun way to affirm your friends is to fill paper bags with candy, an encouraging note from your youth ministry team, and some inspiring verses of Scripture. The outside of the bag is decorated with the name of the student and colorful designs. Simply cut a hole in the top of the bag that is just big enough to slip over a doorknob and you're finished. It can be waiting for them when they come home from school or when they get up.

Roll Out the Red Carpet
When students arrive at your church, have the entire student leadership team out front with a red carpet, chocolate Hugs candies, and lots of high fives to welcome everyone to the meeting.

Ski, Surf, Bike Trips
Fill the weekend with the sport of your choice and the best youth speaker you can find.

curious students
Ideas for spiritual growth—*including small-group ministry, Bible studies, and personal devotional life*

10-Minute All-Night Prayer Meeting
The prayer meeting starts at midnight. Instead of toilet papering houses, go to different areas around your city. At each site spend 10 minutes praying for the people related to that location. Go to each local high school and pray for your friends and teachers. Next, go to your pastor's house and each of your friends' homes and pray for their families.

Gotta Care
Plan your year strategically around the six spiritual disciplines found in **Gotta Care** (see Session 28). They are—

September-October **Pray** | March-April **Tell**
November-December **Give** | May-June **Abide**
January-February **Read the Bible** | July-August **Serve**

(continued)

Concert of Prayer
There are several ways to do a concert of prayer, but to get started, base your time around the P.R.A.Y. prayer. Start your time with worship, Scripture readings, and prayer.

committed students
Ideas for service and leadership—*whether in your church, around your community, out of state, or internationally.*

Service Scavenger Hunt
Throw tradition into reverse for this scavenger hunt. Instead of collecting a list of items, as in a regular scavenger hunt, this one allows you to give. Each team of scavengers is given an identical list of service projects to do. The list could include—wash 10 windows, mow one lawn, raise $10 for a Compassion or World Vision child, and so on. Each project is worth a given amount of points. Teams score points by completing the projects.

Sponsor a Child
A great way to get involved in world relief programs is to sponsor a needy child. Agencies like World Vision and Compassion International link financial sponsors with children overseas. Usually these agencies will ask for a certain amount of money each month to provide food, clothing, and shelter for a particular child. Most of the time, you will receive detailed information about your child, including photos and handwritten thank-you notes from them. The monthly cost to sponsor a child is usually the price of one large pizza and a movie.

Mission Trips
There are mission agencies all around North America. Plan an urban, rural, or cross-cultural mission and allow God to use you in ways you never thought possible.

Big Brother and Big Sister Programs
Challenge your older students to become big brothers or sisters to the younger students coming into your youth ministry. This could be as simple as having your big brothers and sisters get to know the younger students by name and making a point to welcome them each time the group meets. Other ideas include having a big brother and sister invite them to youth events or visit them in their homes. Start small groups with incoming students. Kidnap them for a breakfast before church at the beginning of the year and introduce the year of activities.

10 Unglamorous, Unexotic, Yet Concrete Ways to Serve
1. Mobile soup kitchen
2. Blanket run for the homeless
3. Tele-care phone calls for your entire school
4. Free baby-sitting for the families of the church
5. Adopt a grandparent
6. Adopt an inner city youth group
7. See You At The Pole
8. Campus Bible study
9. Clean up your campus after lunch is over
10. Send flowers to your mom

Program Planning Worksheet

Program _____ Target group _____ Date _____
[*casual, curious,* or *commited* kids?]

Who are the students you expect will attend this event?

Casual student	*Curious* students	*Committed* students
[ready to visit]	[ready to grow]	[ready to serve]

Goals
What do you want to accomplish in this program?

Game Plan
What programming ideas will you use in this program?

Program Schedule

                                         MATERIALS NEEDED   PERSONNEL

- Prep/set-up

- Opening

- The meat of the program

- Wrap-up

The Leadership Program—The Plan, Part Deux

The point
Developing a strategy for the youth ministry.

The point, unwrapped
More about purposeful programming, plus ways to thematically calendar your strategy into your programming.

Where in the Word
Proverbs, John

You'll need—
• ball of yarn (the bigger your leadership team, the bigger the ball of yarn)

Team Building 20 min.

Yarn Sharing Experience
This exercise will get your team talking about their inner feelings and hopes for the coming school year.

Ask your team to stand in a circle. Hold the ball of yarn and explain to the group that they're going to take part in a little experiment. Tell them that in a moment you're going to throw the ball of yarn (while still holding onto the end so the yarn will unwind) to someone in the group.

When that person catches the ball of yarn, he should talk about one of the following—

• What's something you're thankful for?
• Why are you excited about being a student leader this year?
• What has God done for *all* of us?
• How has God answered a specific prayer of yours?

After talking about one of the above, he will throw the ball to someone else in the circle while holding onto the yarn. The next person who catches the ball will also talk about one of the four things above. Keep this going until everyone in the group has had a chance to talk at least once. Several times is best, but this depends on the size of your group and the time you have. After you have made a web-like pattern with the yarn and everyone has had a chance to share, stop the ball and ask them to hold the yarn tight.
Ask your team—

• **What is the yarn doing for us physically?**

• **How are we symbolically held together by the things we shared as we threw the yarn ball around the circle?**

• **What holds a youth ministry together?**

Then ask one or two of the members of the group to drop their hold of the yarn. Immediately the center web becomes loose and the circle widens a little. Then ask—

- **What happens to the group when someone drops his yarn?**

- **What do you think happens to a youth ministry when someone doesn't play her part?**

After you finish the discussion tell everyone to drop their yarn on the count of three. Then have someone pick it up and wind the yarn back into a ball.

You'll need—

- copies of **Nearsighted, Farsighted, or 20/20? All about Vision** (page 198)

- Bibles

- pencils

- Prepared thoughts on why your youth ministry exists, as explained in this section

Team Huddle *10 min.*

You could say to your team—

Just as it took everyone's participation to create that beautiful web-like pattern, it also takes everyone to hold a youth ministry together. And, we need one more "player" to help us hold our youth ministry together—*vision.*

Distribute copies of **Nearsighted, Farsighted, or 20/20? All about Vision** (page 198). Ask one of your student leaders to read Proverbs 29:18 (KJV), which says, "Where there is no vision the people perish."
Ask your team—

- **What is vision?** [It's having a compelling picture of the future, an image that clarifies the purpose of your youth ministry and answers the question, "What business are we in?" or "Why do we exist?"]

- **Where does vision come from?** [Vision begins by seeking God and his Word.]

- **What does the Bible say happens when there is no vision?** [Proverbs 29:18]

- **Why do you think this is true?**

- **What would you say is the vision or purpose of our youth ministry?**

This year we need to gain and maintain a vision for our ministry by focusing on three specific areas: [Encourage students to follow along on their copies of **Nearsighted, Farsighted, or 20/20?** as you summarize the following points]

- **First we need to define our ministry. This is asking the question, *Why do we exist?*** [You'll need to do some work ahead of time to flesh out this section. For example, this would be a great time to share your vision of why you believe your youth ministry exists. If you need further help in this area consult Doug Fields's *Purpose-Driven Youth Ministry.*

  Once you've finished sharing, brainstorm with your students and write a new vision or purpose statement for your youth group.]

- **Second, we need to design our ministry. This is having an overall plan. We'll begin to work on this during the next part of our session.**

- **Third, we need to prepare our ministry. This means carrying out the plan and doing the actual work of ministry. We'll be doing this for the rest of the year.**

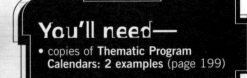

Team Study *20 min.*

Hand out the **Thematic Program Calendars: 2 examples** (page 199) and read through these samples of strategic ways to set up your year with a purpose for spiritual impact. As you go through this process, ask your students from time to time—

- **How well do either of these designs fulfill our vision for our youth ministry?**

- **Which one is closest to what we need? What do we need to tweak? How do we tweak it?**

Make sure students remain positive and concentrate on tweaking ideas, not rejecting other students by rejecting their contributions to the discussion.

Team Prayer *5 min.*

Close your time by inviting God to continue inspiring the team as they seek his vision for the youth ministry, design the youth ministry, and put the plan into action throughout the year.

You'll need—
- copies of **Thematic Program Calendars: 2 examples** (page 199)
- pencils

Nearsighted, Farsighted, or 20/20?

All about Vision

Where there is no vision, the people perish. (Proverbs 29:18)

1. What is vision?

2. Where does vision come from?

3. What do you think the Bible means about having no vision?

4. Why do you think this is true?

5. What would you say is the vision or purpose of our youth ministry?

Three areas to focus on if we're to gain and maintain vision for our youth ministry:

· **Define the ministry**
  Our youth ministry exists to—

· **Design the ministry**

· **Prepare the ministry**

- -

Nearsighted, Farsighted, or 20/20?

All about Vision

Where there is no vision, the people perish. (Proverbs 29:18)

1. What is vision?

2. Where does vision come from?

3. What do you think the Bible means about having no vision?

4. Why do you think this is true?

5. What would you say is the vision or purpose of our youth ministry?

Three areas to focus on if we're to gain and maintain vision for our youth ministry:

· **Define the ministry**
  Our youth ministry exists to—

· **Design the ministry**

· **Prepare the ministry**

Thematic Program Calendars
2 examples

You can design your whole year around the six spiritual disciplines, month to month, or you can simplify and do it quarterly. Or whatever fits your group's needs.

A programming year based on Gotta Care themes

Conceived by Youth for Christ, Gotta Care (www.gottacare.org) is a nationwide campaign intended to get students committed to six pivotal Christian disciplines: praying, giving, reading, witnessing, abiding, and serving. Here are some ideas for each month, based on the campaign's bimonthly themes.

September-October: Gotta Pray

- A concert of prayer
- 10-minute all-night prayer meeting
- See You at the Pole
- Prayer journal
- Prayer triplets
- Prayer breakfast
- 24-hour prayer chain
- Prayer calendar

November-December: Gotta Give

- 30-minute film, documentary, or drama
- Sponsor a child
- Adopt a grandparent in your church or a convalescent home
- Clean up the church day
- Canned food drive and give to local food shelter
- Put together stockings to hand out to children at inner-city housing projects
- Service Scavenger Hunt—Serve people door-to-door rather than asking for things.
- 30-Hour Famine (contact World Vision at www.worldvision.org)

January-February: Gotta Read

- Read the Gospel of John
- Start up Bible studies
- Teach how to have devotions
- Workbooks
- *Experiencing God* by Blackaby & King (Broadman & Holman, 1998)
- *Totally True* by Bill Muir (Youth for Christ, 1991)
- *Just Between God and You* by Bill Muir (Youth for Christ, 1997)
- Memorization of verses (one a week throughout January) John 1:12-13; 3:16; 10:10; 14:5-6

March-April: Gotta Tell

- Challenge each student to sign and pray for their "Bringing My World To Christ" friends.
- Pray the open door prayer
- Teach how to share my faith in any setting
- Special night set aside to pray for spiritually lost friends
- Plan an outreach night: Bring in a band, speaker, testimonies, and an evangelistic call for commitment
- Locker to Locker (sharing the gospel with someone whose locker is next to theirs)
- Invite a friend to Easter Sunday church and share the gospel with them

May-June: Gotta Abide

- Practice the disciplines of prayer, silence, and journaling
- Memorize John 15:1-7
- Sit in the front row of church for the entire two months
- Have lunch with your pastor
- Fast from television and radio for a week and replace it with studying God's Word
- Plan an extended worship night for your youth ministry
- Teach on the temptations we face and how God provides a way of escape.

July-August: Gotta Serve

- Network with existing national and inner-city ministries
- Go on a mission trip
- Pray for a missionary, especially one your students know
- Do a phone hook-up and ask a missionary to talk to your students over the speaker phone. If they have kids, talk with them and pray for them
- Help out at a Back Yard Bible Club or Vacation Bible School
- Set up a secret pal system so that every student in the youth ministry might be encouraged and served

August: *training student leaders to lead campus clubs*
September: *See You at the Pole campaign*
October: *identifying and networking all Christians and Christian clubs on campus*
November: *developing and training evangelism ministry teams, Bible study groups, and discipleship groups*
December: *equipping students for ministry to hurting students and students in crisis*
January: *campus evangelistic event (lock-in, rally, concert, game night, etc.)*
February: *True Love Waits campaign (sexual abstinence emphasis)*
March: *faculty appreciation month*
April: *campus retreat*
May: *follow-up of retreat decisions, and officer election*
June-July: *camp and leadership training (organized by adult youth leaders)*

A programming year based on First Priority themes

The following thematic program calendar is adapted from First Priority's *Student Leader Manual* by Benny Proffitt (Lifeway, 1994).

First Priority (www.christsam bassadors.com/html/body_first-priority.html), by the way, is a multi-denominational network of churches that equips students to establish student-initiated and student-led campus Christian clubs under the guidelines of the Equal Access Act. The stated purpose of club meetings is accountability, outreach and follow-up.

Making Decisions as a Team

The point
Making unified decisions.

The point, unwrapped
Decision-making is a regular task for all leaders, student leaders included. And decisions are often made not by individuals, but by pairs or groups of leaders. So this meeting helps your student leaders discover how to discuss their way into healthy and effective decision-making.

Where in the Word
John, Hebrews

> Making decisions as a group can be a difficult thing for teenagers. It's certainly an issue of understanding the biblical attitudes of gentleness, patience, and humility. But decision-making is also a life skill that takes practice. If you've ever sat in on a church council meeting, you know that many adults haven't developed this skill either. In this session we will look at the biblical view as well as three areas necessary to develop decision-making skills.

Team Building *10 min.*

I'll Take Door Number One
Get a volunteer to come forward and immediately give her a small prize like a candy bar. Ask if she would like to trade her prize for what's behind the door (be creative) or in the box. Make this first trade a good one, such as two passes to a movie or a music CD.

Now ask a group of two to four kids to come forward (if you have a small leadership team, have the entire team play). Their prize just for coming forward should be a candy bar or $1. Again offer to let the group trade the prize in their hand for something behind door number one. If they decide to trade, this time the options should be pretty useless junk, like a broken golf pencil, a fast-food napkin (used or clean), an old 8-track cassette tape, an expired coupon for diapers, and so on. However, the kids won't know this ahead of time and they must decide what to do as a group.

After that group has made their decision and returned to their seats, get another group to come forward to repeat this process. You can decide if the door prize this time is junk or a new car. (It would be fun to have a coupon for a car that you could pull out to show them if they chose not to trade for the door prize!) Again, they must decide—together—whether or not to trade the prize in their hands for something in the box.

Afterward, ask questions like—

- **Why did you choose to trade or keep?**

- **How did it feel to trade for a junky prize?**

- **What was it like to make the decision as a team?**

- **Would you have chosen differently if you were the only one making the choice? Why or why not?**

> ## You'll need—
> - prizes for **I'll Take Door Number One** (candy bar, movie passes, a CD, and some junk)
>
> - a box or "door" for **I'll Take Door Number One**

• **Which do you prefer: making decisions with a group of people or making decisions by yourself? Why?**

• **What are some real-life places where you make decisions with a group of people? What's it like?**

Team Huddle *35 min.*

Distribute **Making Decisions as a Team** (pages 203-204), and have your students form groups to discuss the verses and questions on the handout.
Say something like—

God is very interested in our unity as believers and our attitudes that encourage each other and spur one another on in our faith. Three areas seem to show up in effective leadership teams, and we'd like to get your thoughts on how we're doing in each of these.

Go through the remainder of the handout as a team. You may want to write the three main points on a whiteboard: *Strong teams have 1) a common purpose, 2) leaders who think win-win, and 3) people who are able to listen to one another.*

After mentioning the three points, go over them individually by using the questions on the handout and recording students' answers on the whiteboard. (To add to the discussion about point three, you can refer to the listening skills that were covered in Session 15.)

Team Prayer *10 min.*

Have the students get into groups (or pairs if you have a small group) and pray for each other and the things discussed in this session. Have them pray for unity as they lead. Pray for clarity of purpose, a humble attitude, and courage to listen. You or another selected adult leader could close the group with a prayer for unity.

Making Decisions as a Team

Break into groups to discuss the verses and the following questions.

Read John 17:20-23

1. What seemed to be a major priority to Jesus as he prayed for his followers?

2. Why was this a major priority?

3. What does this say about our need to strive for unity in our leadership team?

4. How are we doing?

Read Hebrews 10:24-25

1. Identify the tasks listed in this section of Scripture.

2. On a scale of 1 to 10 (10 being the highest), how well is our leadership team performing these tasks? Place a mark on each of the three rating scales below.

   Spurring one another on   1 •————————————• 10
   Meeting together   1 •————————————• 10
   Encouraging one another   1 •————————————• 10

3. Why did you rate our team that way?

4. As an individual how are you doing on each of these tasks?

   Spurring one another on   1 •————————————• 10
   Meeting together   1 •————————————• 10
   Encouraging one another   1 •————————————• 10

5. How does each member's performance of these tasks affect the team's ability to perform them?

6. List ways you might need to change if you took these two passages to heart.

7. List ways our team might need to change if we took these two passages to heart.

Strong teams have—
- A common purpose
- Leaders who think win-win
- People who are able to listen to one another

(continued)

Common Purpose

1. What do you think is our primary purpose as a ministry?

2. What is our job as student leaders in accomplishing this purpose?

3. How can understanding this purpose help us be a strong team and make unified decisions?

Win-Win Attitude

1. What does it mean to have a win-win attitude?

2. What are other, less effective attitudes that team members might have?

3. How does having a win-win attitude make the team strong and help it make unified decisions?

4. What does it take to give up a win-lose (or even a lose-lose) perspective?

5. What attitude do you have toward the team and each member of it?

6. What kinds of attitude adjustments might you need to make, and how can you make those adjustments?

Good Listeners

1. What does it take to listen well to others?

2. How does the skill of listening well help build a strong team and enable it to make unified decisions?

3. Are you more of a talker or a listener? Why did you answer that way?

4. What do you need to do to become a better listener?

5. How can we help each other become better listeners?

Unity & Diversity— Dealing with Conflict

The point
Dealing constructively with conflict.

The point, unwrapped
If unity is the goal, conflict is the reality. You can help your student leaders realize the toll of conflict that is unhealthily handled, and the benefits of conflict when it is effectively managed.

Where in the Word
Ephesians, 2 Timothy, James

Team Building *10 min.*

The Fight
Ask for a guy and a girl volunteer. Give them **The Fight** script (page 208) and prepare for a lively exchange. (Note: if you can get this to your actors ahead of time, the skit will turn out even better.)

After the performance, ask your team—

You'll need—
- copies of **The Fight** (page 208)
- two student volunteers

- **What would you advise Isaiah and Mackenna to do? Why?**

- **What basic piece of information seems to be missing from their argument? How is that affecting the conflict?**

- **What mistakes do they each make in how they react to each other? What should they have done instead?**

- **Think of an argument or conflict you've been in recently. What started it?**

- **Do you think you handled the conflict well? Why or why not?**

- **Did you resolve the conflict? If so, how?**

- **If the conflict wasn't resolved, how has the lack of resolution affected your relationship with that person?**

Now explain to your team—

Conflict is part of any relationship, and especially so when you belong to a group. There will be differences of opinions and disagreements on this leadership team that can't be avoided. While conflict can be painful and tough to deal with, it can also be good. Discussing differences and opposing viewpoints can help bring about the best possible solutions and decisions that reflect more than just one or two points of view.

However, God is very concerned about how we treat one another in the process. Let's look at some things that will help us become more effective leaders in this area. First, let's be honest about how we respond to conflict and pray for our time together now.

Team Huddle *15 min.*

Have the group recall times when they were involved in a group decision that was unified and times when it was very divisive. These situations may have been with their friends, in their family (deciding on a vacation spot, for example), at school, or in church.

Make two columns on your whiteboard. Write above one UNITED and above the other DIVIDED. Try to get the students to share brief examples of each and put a key word or words to identify the example in the appropriate column.

Say something like—

You'll need—
• whiteboard and markers

- **What behaviors and attitudes characterized times when you were involved in a united decision?**

- **How did it feel to be on a unified team?**

- **What behaviors and attitudes characterized times when you were involved in a divided decision?**

- **How did it feel to be on a divided team?**

- **What did you learn from these experiences that you'd like to bring to this team?**

Team Study *5 min.*

With your students, go through "**The Rules**" on **Unity/Diversity—Dealing with Conflict** (pages 209-210)
- **Keep a cool head and a tame tongue.** Nothing heats up an argument more that a hot head and a loose tongue. When you disagree, be sure to think before you speak.
- **Be specific.** Generalized statements rarely help. Avoid words like *always* and *never*. Speak to specific situations, actions, and feelings.
- **Keep it focused on you, not them.** If you focus on them, you will end up blaming someone and that always produces defensiveness. Keep your statements personal and use "I" words. For example, "I feel like you don't understand what I'm trying to say. Let me rephrase it."
- **Listen.** The greatest barrier to conflict resolution is the unwillingness or inability to listen. Conversely, the greatest help in dealing with conflict is the ability to listen to the other person. Listen to understand, not to win.
- **Lighten up.** Keep a healthy perspective on things. Don't sweat the small stuff. It usually isn't that big of a deal.
- **Stick to the facts.** Do whatever you can to be focused in your discussions. Don't get sidetracked or caught up in any personal attacks.

You'll need—
• copies of **Unity/Diversity—Dealing with Conflict** (pages 209-210)
• Bibles
• pencils

Ask your students if they can think of any examples to illustrate each point. Also ask them if they've had any personal experiences where these rules were or weren't used during a conflict and have them share with the group what happened in either case.

Now have the students complete and then discuss each section of the **Unity/Diversity—Dealing with Conflict** handout (pages 209-210) in small groups. Wrap up with a large group discussion of the highlights in the study.

Say something like—

Here's a tough question, but one we need to deal with honestly. Do we need to address any conflicts within our group right now?

If students answer positively, follow up by asking—

- **What is the conflict about?**

- **How can we apply the rules of clean conflict and what we learned in Scripture to resolve this conflict?**

If you can't resolve the conflict right away, set aside a specific time to deal with it soon. Encourage students to pray that God would prepare them and their teammates to resolve the conflict in a way that honors him.

Team Prayer *5-10 min.*

End your session in conversational prayer. You might try having each person pray about something they learned during this session. Have them ask God for strength to have the right attitude in the midst of conflict, whether at home, at school, or in this leadership team. You can close the session with a prayer for unity.

The Fight

The Scene
A boyfriend and girlfriend get into a ridiculous argument.

Cast
Isaiah

Mackenna

(Mackenna is sitting, fuming. Isaiah enters, relieved to finally find her)

ISAIAH: *(entering)* There you are. I've been looking all over the place for you. *(No response from Mackenna)* What's wrong? *(No response from Mackenna)* Are you gonna tell me what's wrong, or just sit there and ignore me?

MACKENNA: Do I really have to tell you? Do I?

ISAIAH: Well…yeah.

MACKENNA: Ha! If I have to tell you, then you don't deserve to know.

ISAIAH: Come again?

MACKENNA: You're telling me you don't know. I can't believe you don't know. How could you not know?

ISAIAH: I don't know how I don't know. I just don't!

MACKENNA: That figures. My mom's right. You guys are all alike. You're just like my dad.

ISAIAH: You don't have to get nasty.

MACKENNA: Oh, now you insult my dad!

ISAIAH: No, *you* did!

MACKENNA: That's because he's my dad. You just watch what you say.

ISAIAH: Look, Mackenna, what do you want? I'm no mind reader. You're either going to have to tell me what's wrong, or…

MACKENNA: Or what?

ISAIAH: Or I'll leave.

MACKENNA: You would, wouldn't you?

ISAIAH: I don't want to, but I don't know what else to do.

MACKENNA: Fine. Leave.

ISAIAH: *(Getting up to exit)* Okay, I'll leave.

MACKENNA: *(Getting up to exit)* Better yet—I'll leave.

ISAIAH: *(Moving to exit)* Forget it. I will.

MACKENNA: *(Moving to exit)* I'm leaving. You stay still.

ISAIAH: *(Exiting)* No way. I'm gone.

MACKENNA: *(Exiting)* See ya. I've already left.

ISAIAH: *(Exits)* Girls!

MACKENNA: *(Exits)* Guys!

Unity/Diversity—
Dealing with Conflict

The rules

- **Keep a cool head and a tame tongue.** Nothing heats up an argument more that a hot head and a loose tongue. When you disagree, be sure to think before you speak.
- **Be specific.** Generalized statements rarely help. Avoid words like always and never. Speak to specific situations, actions, and feelings.
- **Keep it focused on you, not them.** If you focus on them, you will end up blaming someone and that always produces defensiveness. Keep your statements personal and use "I" words. For example, "I feel like you don't understand what I'm trying to say. Let me rephrase it."
- **Listen.** The greatest barrier to conflict resolution is the unwillingness or inability to listen. Conversely, the greatest help in dealing with conflict is the ability to listen to the other person. Listen to understand, not to win.
- **Lighten up.** Keep a healthy perspective on things. Don't sweat the small stuff. It usually isn't that big of a deal.
- **Stick to the facts.** Do whatever you can to be focused in your discussions. Don't get sidetracked or caught up in any personal attacks.

The discussion

1. How can these guidelines help our team deal with conflict in a constructive, not destructive, way?

2. Are there other guidelines you would add to this list? If so, what are they?

3. Which of these guidelines is the hardest for you to follow during a conflict? Why?

4. How can we encourage each other to keep our conflicts clean?

Read and answer—
- Ephesians 4:25-32
- 2 Timothy 2:23-24
- James 4:1-3.

(continued)

5. According to Ephesians 4:25-32, what attitudes and actions should we adopt to help us have clean conflicts? What attitudes and actions should we avoid?

6. What do you think is the difference between *arguments* and *quarrels* in 2 Timothy 2:23-24?

7. What's a modern-day example of an *argument*? Of a *quarrel*?

8. What does this 2 Timothy passage say about how God's servants should and should not interact with others?

9. According to James 4:1-3, what often lies behind fights and quarrels?

10. What do all of these passages teach us about handling conflicts on our team?

11. Based on these passages, should we add anything to or reword any of our rules for clean conflicts?

Evaluating Your Ministry

The point
Student leaders will evaluate the effectiveness of the youth ministry program.

The point, unwrapped
Evaluation is critically important if a group wants to determine its effectiveness. So in this meeting, student leaders will practice assessing their youth ministry program.

Team Building *5 minutes*
Welcome students and ask one of them to open up in prayer. Introduce the tool you will be using: either **Meeting/Event Evaluation** (pages 212-213) or the **Year-End Wrap-Up Evaluation** (pages 214-215).

How to use the Meeting/Event Evaluation
Meeting/Event Evaluation (page 213) is perfect after a meeting or an event. Best-case scenario is to take a few minutes after each event and debrief. This kind of evaluation shows you what you did right and what needs improvement. Invite your students to express their thoughts of praise and concern.

Thinking through the questions
The questions will help your students think about what worked well and what to improve.
- Question **1** starts the whole time off positively. Share stories of what God is doing in the lives of students and leaders in your group. Don't go past this point without sharing a few stories of life change.
- Question **2** identifies the areas that were winners.
- Question **3** identifies problem areas in the program and what to do about them.
- Questions **4** and **5** will give you an idea if your ministry is outwardly open and friendly or inwardly closed and cliquish.
- Question **6** will challenge the team to pray.

You'll need—
- copies of the desired **Evaluating Our Ministry** evaluation tools: **Meeting/Event Evaluation** (page 213) or **Year-End Wrap-Up Evaluation** (pages 214)
- pencils

How to use the Year-End Wrap-Up Evaluation
The end of the year is a perfect time to evaluate everything that has taken place. **Year End Wrap-Up Evaluation** (page 214) shows what you have been doing right and what needs improvement. Invite your students to express their thoughts of praise and concern. This questionnaire can also be helpful in launching a planning meeting.

Thinking through the questions
- Question **2** gives valuable insight into the spiritual development of your group.
- Question **3** identifies problem areas in your church's program.
- Question **4** can tell you what you did that was a winner.

- Questions **5** and **6** tell you what events to plan and what subjects to tackle.
- Pay attention to question **10**. Note the names given here, especially if they're repeated. These are the kids to encourage in leadership roles. Let them know that others look up to them.
- Question **11** should be taken seriously. See what you can do to implement the ideas offered.

Team Huddle *15-20 min.*

Evaluating Our Ministry

Say to your team words to this effect—

We're going to take some time to evaluate and assess where we are right now in our ministry. Periodically we want to take the time to see if we're hitting or missing the mark as a student leadership team.

Hand out the evaluation tool you wish to use at this time and give students time to work on their own. After the students are finished, spend some time listening and reflecting on where you are and where you need to go.

Team Prayer

Close in prayer and praise God for the good work he is doing in the ministry. Pray for wisdom for the next steps.

Meeting/event evaluation

Meeting/event _____

Date _____

Number in attendance _____

Purpose of the event _____

1. Share some stories about good things that happened among the students attending.

2. What worked well at this event?
- Did we accomplish the purpose of this meeting? If so, how did we do it?

- On a scale from seven to 863, how prepared were we for this event? Please add your comments.

- What did we do to make sure our materials were available and ready to use?

- What did we do to publicize the event well?

- On a scale from 19 to 524, how possible did we make it to transport everyone to and from this meeting? Please add your comments.

- Other comments:

3. How could we improve upon this event in the future?

4. Were students excited to bring their unchurched friends to this event? Why or why not?

5 On a scale from four to 444, how welcome did people feel at this meeting? Explain your rating.

6. Did we remember to pray for the event? Explain your answer.

7. Did anyone become a Christian during the event? Who? How should we follow up?

8. Other comments:

Evaluation completed by _____

From *Student Leadership Training Manual* by Dennis "Tiger" McLuen & Chuck Wysong. Permission to reproduce this page granted only for use in the buyer's own youth group. www.YouthSpecialties.com

Year-end wrap-up evaluation

Age _____ Grade _____ Male _____ Female _____

1. How long have you been attending our youth ministry?

2. What have you discovered about God this year?

3. You attend worship service at our church: (*circle one*) regularly/fairly often/sometimes/not often (If you circled sometimes or not often, let us know why you do not attend on a regular basis.)

4. What activities did you enjoy the most this year?

5. What events or programs would you like to see us do next year?

6. What topics or subjects would you like us to discuss or teach during the coming year?

7. How would you like to be involved in the coming year?

8. Would you like a chance to teach or speak in front of other kids? If yes, please give us some ideas for topics that you'd like to teach or speak about.

9. If you had a problem during the year, which of our staff people would you probably talk to about it? Why?

10. Name two or three students in our youth ministry who seem to be good examples of what a Christian should be (add a little explanation as to why these people are good examples):
    •
    •
    •

11. On the back of this paper, please write any suggestions you think would improve our church or youth ministry in the year to come.

More resourses for your student leaders

September 29, 2005

Dear Luis,

Here at Bayside Community Church, we're serious about creating opportunities for students to be involved in leadership. As you know, we have student leaders involved in a wide variety of ministries. Students are crucial to our ministry, and we would like you to consider being a part of the student leadership team.

We have the following opportunities:

- Greeter
- Program planning administrator
- Program planning team member
- Small group discipleship leader
- Worship leader

Read the enclosed student leadership commitment sheet, and prayerfully consider whether you can commit to this opportunity. Be sure to consider the expectations and the time that will be required. If you want to pursue this leadership opportunity, fill out the application and return it to me by October 10, 2005.

After I have your application, I will get in touch with you to set up a brief interview. You will know whether you have been accepted one week after the interview.

If you have any questions, give me a call. Student leaders are a crucial part of our ministry here, and I really hope you will seriously consider joining our team.

Sincerely in Christ,

Marcus Heskett
Pastor to Students

From *Student Leadership Training Manual* by Dennis "Tiger" McLuen & Chuck Wysong. Permission to reproduce this page granted only for use in the buyer's own youth group. www.YouthSpecialties.com

217

Student Leadership Expectations

Don't let anyone look down on you because you are young, but set an example for the believers in speech, in life, in love, in faith and in purity.   1 Timothy 4:12

Spiritual expectations
• I acknowledge that I have a personal relationship with Jesus Christ.
• I desire to serve God with my whole life.
• I am committed to spiritual growth through individual and group study.
• I am willing to be involved actively in my church through attendance and attitude.

Behavioral expectations
• I am serious about my lifestyle because I know it tells other people about my commitment to Christ.
• I am committed to a lifestyle made up of choices that honor God.
• I am willing to remain teachable and willing to grow in my faith.

Leadership expectations
• I am committing to a particular student leadership ministry area and will be consistent in that area.
• I am willing to attend youth ministry events and greet visitors at those events.
• I will attend all required student leadership training events and retreats.
• I am willing to meet with an adult mentor on a regular basis.
• I understand and am willing to work within the youth ministry vision statement.
• I am committing to a positive role in our youth ministry in my behavior and attitudes.

Ministry commitments
I commit to work in the following student leadership areas: (check one or more)
    ❏ Youth Board
    ❏ Peer Evangelism Team
    ❏ Worship Team
    ❏ Small Group Leader
    ❏ Children's Church
    ❏ Servant Team
    ❏ Drama Group
    ❏ _____
    ❏ _____
    ❏ _____

_____   _____
              student signature   date

_____
              parent signature

Student Leadership Application

Name _____ Age_____ Grade_____

Address _____

Phone _____ School _____

1. Why do you want to be in student leadership?

2. Describe your relationship to Christ, including some high points that have helped you get to where you are today.

3. How has this church helped you spiritually?

4. What strengths do you bring to the student leadership team?

5. List two weaknesses you need to work on.

6. List the school activities you're involved in.

7. List the nonschool activities you're involved in (job, clubs, etc.).

8. Will any of these cause a schedule problem for you? Please explain.

9. Any comments or questions?

Youth Board Duties and Responsibilities

Don't let anyone look down on you because you are young, but set an example for the believers in speech, in life, in love, in faith and in purity. 1 Timothy 4:12

The youth board member shall—

- Express personal faith in Jesus Christ.

- Share responsibility for the youth ministry program at _____

church name

- Plan all youth activities, in coordination with the youth pastor.

- Assist the youth pastor in the implementation of the youth events.

- Demonstrate leadership among peers.

- Be a primary input mechanism for the youth pastor—that is, share ideas and suggestions from other youth group members and also relay information from the youth pastor to the youth group.

- Demonstrate enthusiasm and support for planned events by, welcoming new people at events, inviting friends to events, and praying for the youth ministry.

- Attend annual youth board retreats.

- Attend monthly meetings.

- Demonstrate a willingness to learn and grow in the Christian faith.

- Assist in record-keeping on visitors.

Servant Team Job Descriptions

Welcome Team
- Welcome people at youth group events; talk with them.
- Provide name tags for people at selected events.
- Record visitors' names on the welcome team chart.

Follow-Up Team
- Get visitor cards and make sure all new people are invited to come again.
- Keep a list of all new people and their progress toward becoming an active member.
- Send a card to the new students during the week following their first visits.

Scenic Engineering Team
- Set up before events.
- Clean up after events and have a staff person lock-up.
- Decorate the room for special events.

Refreshment Team
- Organize refreshments at selected events.
- Be in charge of birthday treats.

Mission Team
- Help plan and publicize the mission trip.
- Organize local mission efforts.
- Plan mission reports.
- Work with the youth pastor to decide locations and dates of mission trips.

Photography/Media Team
- Take pictures of selected youth events.
- Organize media shows for selected youth events.
- Put up pictures in the youth room following each major event.
- Provide monthly updates on the youth ministry bulletin board.
- Develop a youth group yearbook.

Telephone Contact Team
- Call new or fringe people and invite them to events.
- Work with the Follow-Up Team when necessary.
- Develop a phone chain to communicate information or prayer needs to the youth group.

Newsletter/Publicity Team
- Design, write, and mail a monthly newsletter or calendar.
- Plan creative ways to publicize youth group events.
- Use the youth ministry bulletin board to promote upcoming events.
- Present a weekly promotional time in the youth group meeting.

Fundraising Team
- Manage the Sunday school offerings.
- Manage offerings for the youth group's fundraising events.

Tips for Leading a Meeting

- Start on time.
- Prepare before the meeting starts. Know what the purpose of the meeting is going to be and let the group know. If the agenda involves a lot of items, print out copies of it for your team members.
- Think hard about how you will begin and end the meeting. Both of these are crucial to the success of a meeting. Design an appropriate introduction, and always end the meeting—don't just let it fizzle.
- Don't stay on a sick horse. Be willing to move on if what you're doing isn't working.
- Notice the people, not just the agenda. The key to a good meeting is the people—the leader needs to notice who is or isn't participating.
- Vary the activities.
- Better to end too soon than to drag a meeting out too long.
- Be a good listener as well as a good leader.
- Be a positive leader.

Tips for Leading a Small Group Discussion

- Be a good listener.
- Affirm people and encourage participation.
- Don't be afraid to direct questions to individuals.
- Make sure ground rules are clear from the beginning.
- Be aware of the physical setting. (Are people facing each other? Is the room too large for the group? Are there enough seats for all members? Are there distractions?)
- Prepare your discussion questions and have more questions than you'll need.
- Avoid using all true-false, right-wrong, or yes-no questions.
- Be prepared.
- Lead the people, not just the meeting.
- Be committed to the members of the group.
- Be committed to praying for the members of the group.
- If you ask a question and they look puzzled, rephrase it and ask again.
- Affirm answers and keep drawing group members into the discussion.
- Focus on the group, not on yourself.
- Encourage people to get involved and respond to what is being said. Invite more than one answer.
- Don't let one person monopolize the conversation.
- Move from light to heavy discussion.
- Call people by name.

Tips for Leading Music and Worship

- Practice is essential. Lack of preparation is not the key to spontaneity.
- Meet with the musicians beforehand to go over last minute details.
- Pray.
- Be sure all musicians have a copy of the music or schedule.
- Remember that your job is to help facilitate singing and worship, not just perform.
- Be positive and encouraging.
- If the group doesn't know the song, be sure to teach them and then invite them into the experience. Your job is to get them involved.
- Don't use only one style or tempo of music.
- Talk about how to focus on the music and the worship, not on ourselves.
- Be sure the sound system is clear but not overpowering the musicians. Just because the worship team is singing, it doesn't ensure the atmosphere of group worship.

Tips for Leading Games

- Make sure you have all the materials needed for the game.
- Tell the group the basic idea and point of the game.
- Work hard on clear, concise directions. Practice them if needed. It will kill the energy if people don't understand how to play the game or if the directions take forever to explain.
- Demonstrate the game briefly so participants can see what you want.
- Have fun.
- Choose games that invite participation and are age-appropriate.
- Stop before the energy is drained. It's always better to end a game when participants would like more time, than to end it 15 minutes after everyone wishes it had ended.
- Minimize the competitive elements.
- Choose games that fit the size of your group.

Student Leader Overnighter

The sessions in *Student Leadership Training Manual* have been designed so that if you want a more intense time of training, you can lead many of these meetings during a student-leader overnighter. Since you can't teach the entire curriculum in one weekend, plan to teach only a set of related sessions—10-12 (devotional life), 15-17 (peer ministry), 18-21 (evangelism), etc. Of course, mix and match different sessions to meet whatever leadership needs your team has.

The Question Game

Each student and leader is given two small pieces of paper and asked to write a thought-provoking question on each of them, such as:

- When was the last time you cried and why?

- Which student in this room do you admire the most and why?

- If you could be anyone in the Bible except Jesus, who would you be and why?

All the questions are put into a hat; the students draw and answer them at random. After each question is answered, the person who responded then passes the hat to the person of their choosing. Complete at least two rounds. Encourage students and adults to be as honest as they can, but remember that not all of them will be on the same level of intimacy.

Sample schedule

Friday

7:00 p.m.	Arrive at the designated location
7:30 p.m.	Session 1: Becoming a Leader
8:30 p.m.	Snack time—pizza is delivered!
9:00 p.m.	Session 27: The Leadership Program—The Plan
10:45 p.m.	The Question Game (at left)
12:00 a.m.	Lights out (Yeah, right....okay, instead show *Mr. Holland's Opus* with lots of popcorn and tissues.)

Saturday

8:00 a.m.	Breakfast
8:30 a.m.	Quiet time: Matthew 28:18-20
9:00 a.m.	Session 18: Developing a Heart for Lost People
10:00 a.m.	Snack time
10:30 a.m.	Session 19: Sharing Your Faith with Your Friends
11:45 a.m.	Fix up your ugly youth room! (posters, bulletin board overhaul, and so on)
12:30 p.m.	Break for lunch—see ya Sunday!

Mini Prayer Retreat

This two-hour Mini Prayer Retreat is intended to—
- Give the leadership team a basic understanding of the different elements of prayer
- Let them experience four types of prayer
- Get them excited about spending time in prayer
- Introduce them to the Hand Illustration as a tool for intercessory prayer
- Allow the team to spend time praying together as a group

This prayer retreat teaches youth how to pray not through lectures, discussions, books, or videos, but by actually praying. The experience may raise some questions among the participants about prayer, but rather than answering these during the retreat, discuss them individually at a later time or during one of your leadership meetings.

In order to make the prayer retreat more successful, encourage everyone to get plenty of sleep the week before. Also tell the students to use a lot of variety during their time of individual prayer. Encourage them to sit a while, walk around, stand, kneel, read Scripture, write prayers, sit in silence, and pray aloud. Ask them to try to spend the last five minutes of each part of the retreat in silence, listening to God.

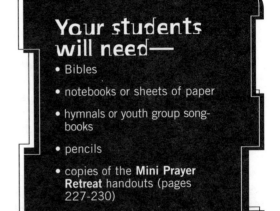

Your students will need—
- Bibles
- notebooks or sheets of paper
- hymnals or youth group songbooks
- pencils
- copies of the **Mini Prayer Retreat** handouts (pages 227-230)
- copies of church and youth group attender prayer requests, prepared before the retreat

Gathering *15 min.*

Hand out a prayer request list with requests from the church and the youth group that have been gathered ahead of time. Go over the schedule and procedure for the prayer retreat. Before beginning the individual time of prayer, briefly go over the following description of the different parts of prayer.

P-R-A-Y
The letters of the word PRAY can be used as an acrostic to help you remember four types of prayer: praise, repentance, asking for others, asking for yourself. Prayer should never become routine or planned, but there are certain types of prayer that we should incorporate into our prayer times.

Praise and thanksgiving
The time we spend talking with God should begin with a time of praise (worshiping God for who he is) and thanksgiving (thanking God for the things he has done for us and for the blessings he has given to us).

Try keeping a list of things you discover about God that you can praise him for and Bible passages that contain praises as well as a "Things I Thank God For" list that includes everything that comes to your mind you're thankful for. This list can be used during your prayer time to praise and thank God.

Repentance

"If I had cherished sin in my heart, the Lord would not have listened," wrote the psalmist in Psalm 66:18-20, "but God has surely listened and heard my voice in prayer. Praise be to God, who has not rejected my prayer or withheld his love from me!"

When we go to God in prayer, we need to ask him to show us where we have sinned—and then ask him to forgive those things.

Asking for others

This is the time in our prayers when we pray for other people's needs. As people mention prayer requests in the worship service at church, at a youth group meeting, or just in conversation, we should write those requests down so we remember to pray for them. The prayers we pray for other people *do* make a difference.

Asking for Yourself

"Cast all your anxiety on him because he cares for you," wrote the apostle in 1 Peter 5:7. God wants us to share our hurts and our sorrows with him. He wants us to tell him our needs and ask him for guidance. He is concerned about our relationships, our schoolwork, our dreams, and our fears. He is concerned because he loves us. He wants, more than anything, for us to spend time with him, sharing from the depths of our hearts.

After going through this information, send each participant to a private room or location where they will stay for the next couple hours and go through the procedure outlined on the Mini Prayer Retreat pages (parts one through four) that follow (pages 227-230).

Closing *25 min.*
Have everyone come back together for a time of group prayer and sharing.

Praise and thanksgiving

Worship God for who he is and thanking him for all he has done for us

(25 minutes)

Praise

Let everything that has breath praise the Lord. —Psalm 150:6

1. Look up the following Scriptures and praise God for the things you discover about him in each Scripture:

1 Chronicles 29:10-13	Isaiah 25:1	John 1:29	Hebrews 1:2-3
Psalm 23	Isaiah 66:1-2	John 8:12	1 Peter 2:24
Psalm 89:11	Jeremiah 32:17	Philippians 2:9-11	Revelation 1:8
Psalm 116:5, 8	Matthew 28:18	Philippians 4:19	Revelation 4:11
Psalm 139:1-6	John 1:1, 14	1 Timothy 6:15	Revelation 5:13

2. The last seven psalms in the Bible (Psalms 144-150) are all psalms of praise to God. Read through one or two of these psalms and try to find the reason the psalmist is praising God. Then spend time praising God for the same reasons the psalmist did.

3. Spend time reading aloud (or singing) several praise songs to God from the hymnal or youth group songbook.

Thanksgiving

Enter his gates with thanksgiving and his courts with praise; give thanks to him and praise his name. —Psalm 100:4

1. Make a "Things I'm Thankful For" list. On it list as many things as you can think of that you are thankful for. Suggestions to get you started:

• Jesus' love	• A home	• Freedom	• Education
• Family	• Your youth group	• Opportunities	• Food
• Health	• God's forgiveness	• Friends	• The Bible

2. Once your list is completed, talk to God and tell him how thankful you are for each of the things on the list. If *freedom* is on your list, for example, and you're not sure how to pray thanksgiving for it, you can simply read this to God as a prayer:

Lord, I thank you for all the freedoms I have in this country and especially for the freedom to worship. I realize that not everyone in the world has these same freedoms, and I ask you to help me never to take them for granted and to always be grateful and thankful to you for all of them.

From *Student Leadership Training Manual* by Dennis "Tiger" McLuen & Chuck Wysong. Permission to reproduce this page granted only for use in the buyer's own youth group. www.YouthSpecialties.com

227

3. Spend time in silence listening to God and letting him show you things you have to praise him for and things you have to be thankful for.

Mini Prayer Retreat

Repentance

Admitting to God that you have sinned and asking him to forgive you and help you overcome it
(25 minutes)

If we confess our sins, he is faithful and just and will forgive us our sins and purify us from all unrighteousness.

—1 John 1:9

1. Read Psalm 51. King David wrote this prayer to God after he had been convicted of his sin of adultery. As you read the Psalm, you can almost feel David's broken heart and understand God's loving forgiveness.

2. Spend time praying and asking God to show you the things in your life that are not in line with his will for your life. Make a list of the things he shows you.

3. Now go through each item on your list and ask God to forgive you and help you have the desire and strength to overcome them.

4. Spend time in silence listening to God. Let him speak to your heart and tell you how much he loves you and forgives you. As you listen accept his forgiveness and feel his cleansing.

Asking for others

Interceding or praying for other people and their needs
(30 minutes)

Therefore confess your sins to each other and pray for each other so that you may be healed. The prayer of a righteous man is powerful and effective.

—James 5:16

1. If it's helpful, you can use this graphic reminder to pray for the things that come to your heart for each of the following groups of people:

When you look at your hand, the closest finger (although it isn't technically a finger) is our thumb. When you pray, let your thumb remind you to pray for the people who are closest to you—family, friends, fellow athletes, or someone in your drama club.

Your pointer finger should remind you to pray for the people who point the way for you. This could be your pastor, youth leader, coach, teachers, or others who try to point you in the right direction.

Let the middle finger, the tallest finger, represent those who are over you in leadership positions. These would be the governmental leaders of your town, your state, and your country.

The people closest to you

People who point the way for you

Those in leadership positions at all levels

People who are weak and in need

Yourself

Your ring finger is the weakest finger you have, and it should remind you to pray for those you know who are weak or in need. This could include people you know who are—

▫ Sick ▫ Addicted to drugs or alcohol ▫ Going through family struggles ▫ Having financial problems ▫ Experiencing emotional problems ▫ In trouble with the law ▫ Homeless

Your little finger represents yourself.

When you come to the time in your prayers each day when you are praying for people, let the fingers on your hand remind you of all the people you need to pray for.

Now spend some time praying for each of these groups of people. You'll deal with your personal needs during the next part of this retreat.

Mini Prayer Retreat

Yourself
(30 minutes)

Don't worry about anything; instead, pray about everything; tell God your needs and don't forget to thank him for his answers. If you do this you will experience God's peace, which is far more wonderful than the human mind can understand. —Philippians 4:6-7 (*Living Bible*)

1. Begin by writing out a Worry List below. It should be a list of everything that you are currently worried about or things that are bugging you. Every concern you have in the world should be listed here:

2. Once you have made your list, read it over and divide the items into two separate categories. In Category 1 include the items you can do something about. Beside each item in this category, write down what you can do. This first category of worries now becomes a **To -do list** that you can take home and begin to work on. Ask God to give you the strength and wisdom to do the things you know you need to do.

In Category 2 include items you can do nothing about. These things are completely out of your control. This second category of worries now becomes your **Personal prayer list**. Spend time talking with God

To-do list	What I can do about this	Personal prayer

about each item on the list. Tell him about your needs and leave them with him.

3. Spend time in silence listening to God. Let him teach you what steps you can take to deal with the items on your **To-do list** and give you a sense of peace about the items on your **Personal prayer list** that you can do nothing about.

Education that fits your schedule.

Graduate Program

- Youth Leadership offers a youth ministry concentration for both the M.A. and M. Div. degrees in cooperation with Luther and Bethel Seminaries in St. Paul, Minnesota.

- We offer two models to receive these degrees:
  The Traditional Program
  The Distance Learning Program

Distance Learning

- Stay in your current ministry and receive a seminary degree in youth and family ministry.

- Attend intensive classes twice a year, take courses on the computer, and interact through a virtual classroom and discussion folders.

Traditional Program

- Come to seminary and receive the most complete youth ministry program available.

- Each student receives a personal education mentor.

- 2-year paid internships.

Youth Ministry Institute

- With Youth Leadership's Institutes you can attend a one-week graduate level course in youth ministry. Excellent instruction, in-depth application, and personal interaction. Enroll for continuing education or graduate credit.

- Institutes are scheduled annually for February in San Diego, CA, and for July in St. Paul, MN.

- Courses offered include:
  Foundations of Youth Ministry
  Pastoral Care of Youth
  Leadership and Management Skills
  Communicating the Gospel to Teenagers
  Youth Ministry in Urban Settings

"The Youth Leadership combination of theological education and practical experience is unmatched in the field of youth ministry."

Dennis "Tiger" McLuen,
Executive Director

Youth Leadership
122 West Franklin Ave. - Suite 510
Minneapolis, MN 55404
(800) 755-LEAD or, (612) 870-3632
www.youthleadership.org
ythlead@aol.com

Our Mission
"To equip adults and churches to more effectivly share the good news of Jesus Christ with teenagers and their famililes."

Resources from Youth Specialties

Youth Ministry Programming

Camps, Retreats, Missions, & Service Ideas
(Ideas Library)

Compassionate Kids: Practical Ways to Involve
Your Students in Mission and Service

Creative Bible Lessons from the Old Testament

Creative Bible Lessons in 1 & 2 Corinthians

Creative Bible Lessons in John: Encounters
with Jesus

Creative Bible Lessons in Romans: Faith
on Fire!

Creative Bible Lessons on the Life of Christ

Creative Bible Lessons in Psalms

Creative Junior High Programs from A to Z,
Vol. 1 (A-M)

Creative Junior High Programs from A to Z,
Vol. 2 (N-Z)

Creative Meetings, Bible Lessons, & Worship
Ideas (Ideas Library)

Crowd Breakers & Mixers (Ideas Library)

Downloading the Bible Leader's Guide

Drama, Skits, & Sketches (Ideas Library)

Drama, Skits, & Sketches 2 (Ideas Library)

Dramatic Pauses

Everyday Object Lessons

Games (Ideas Library)

Games 2 (Ideas Library)

Great Fundraising Ideas for Youth Groups

More Great Fundraising Ideas for Youth Groups

Great Retreats for Youth Groups

Holiday Ideas (Ideas Library)

Hot Illustrations for Youth Talks

More Hot Illustrations for Youth Talks

Still More Hot Illustrations for Youth Talks

Ideas Library on CD-ROM

Incredible Questionnaires for Youth Ministry

Junior High Game Nights

More Junior High Game Nights

Kickstarters: 101 Ingenious Intros to Just
about Any Bible Lesson

Live the Life! Student Evangelism Training Kit

Memory Makers

The Next Level Leader's Guide

Play It! Over 150 Great Games for
Youth Groups

Roaring Lambs

Special Events (Ideas Library)

Spontaneous Melodramas

Student Leadership Training Manual

Student Underground: An Event Curriculum on
the Persecuted Church

Super Sketches for Youth Ministry

Talking the Walk

Teaching the Bible Creatively

Videos That Teach

What Would Jesus Do? Youth Leader's Kit

Wild Truth Bible Lessons

Wild Truth Bible Lessons 2

Wild Truth Bible Lessons—Pictures of God

Worship Services for Youth Groups

Professional Resources

Administration, Publicity, & Fundraising
(Ideas Library)

Equipped to Serve: Volunteer Youth Worker
Training Course

Help! I'm a Junior High Youth Worker!

Help! I'm a Small-Group Leader!

Help! I'm a Sunday School Teacher!

Help! I'm a Volunteer Youth Worker!

How to Expand Your Youth Ministry

How to Speak to Youth...and Keep Them
Awake at the Same Time

Junior High Ministry (Updated & Expanded)

The Ministry of Nurture: A Youth Worker's
Guide to Discipling Teenagers

Purpose-Driven Youth Ministry

Purpose-Driven Youth Ministry Training Kit

So That's Why I Keep Doing This! 52
Devotional Stories for Youth Workers

A Youth Ministry Crash Course

The Youth Worker's Handbook to
Family Ministry

Discussion Starters

Discussion & Lesson Starters (Ideas Library)

Discussion & Lesson Starters 2 (Ideas Library)

EdgeTV

Get 'Em Talking

Keep 'Em Talking!

High School TalkSheets

More High School TalkSheets

High School TalkSheets: Psalms and Proverbs

Junior High TalkSheets

More Junior High TalkSheets

Junior High TalkSheets: Psalms and Proverbs

Real Kids: Short Cuts

Real Kids: The Real Deal—on Friendship,
Loneliness, Racism, & Suicide

Real Kids: The Real Deal—on Sexual Choices,
Family Matters, & Loss

Real Kids: The Real Deal—on Stressing Out,
Addictive Behavior, Great Comebacks,
& Violence

Real Kids: Word on the Street

Unfinished Sentences: 450 Tantalizing
Statement-Starters to Get Teenagers
Talking & Thinking

What If...? 450 Thought-Provoking Questions
to Get Teenagers Talking, Laughing,
and Thinking

Would You Rather...? 465 Provocative
Questions to Get Teenagers Talking

Have You Ever...? 450 Intriguing Questions
Guaranteed to Get Teenagers Talking

Art Source Clip Art

Stark Raving Clip Art (print)

Youth Group Activities (print)

Clip Art Library Version 2.0 (CD-ROM)

Digital Resources

Clip Art Library Version 2.0 (CD-ROM)

Ideas Library on CD-ROM

Videos & Video Curricula

EdgeTV

Equipped to Serve: Volunteer Youth Worker
Training Course

The Heart of Youth Ministry: A Morning with
Mike Yaconelli

Live the Life! Student Evangelism Training Kit

Purpose-Driven Youth Ministry Training Kit

Real Kids: Short Cuts

Real Kids: The Real Deal—on Friendship,
Loneliness, Racism, & Suicide

Real Kids: The Real Deal—on Sexual Choices,
Family Matters, & Loss

Real Kids: The Real Deal—on Stressing Out,
Addictive Behavior, Great Comebacks,
& Violence

Real Kids: Word on the Street

Student Underground: An Event Curriculum on
the Persecuted Church

Understanding Your Teenager Video Curriculum

Student Resources

Downloading the Bible: A Rough Guide to the
New Testament

Downloading the Bible: A Rough Guide to the
Old Testament

Grow For It Journal

Grow For It Journal through the Scriptures

Spiritual Challenge Journal: The Next Level

Teen Devotional Bible

What Would Jesus Do? Spiritual
Challenge Journal

Wild Truth Journal for Junior Highers

Wild Truth Journal—Pictures of God

LINCOLN CHRISTIAN COLLEGE AND SEMINARY